UKRAINE
DIARY

UKRAINE DIARY

Henri J. M. Nouwen

ORBIS BOOKS
Maryknoll, New York 10545

Founded in 1970, Orbis Books endeavors to publish works that enlighten the mind, nourish the spirit, and challenge the conscience. The publishing arm of the Maryknoll Fathers and Brothers, Orbis seeks to explore the global dimensions of the Christian faith and mission, to invite dialogue with diverse cultures and religious traditions, and to serve the cause of reconciliation and peace. The books published reflect the views of their authors and do not represent the official position of the Maryknoll Society. To learn more about Maryknoll and Orbis Books, please visit our website at www.orbisbooks.com.

Library of Congress Cataloging-in-Publication Data

Library of Congress Cataloging-in-Publication Data

Names: Nouwen, Henri J. M., author. | Gudziak, Borys, writer of introduction.
Title: Ukraine diary / Henri J.M. Nouwen.
Description: Maryknoll, NY : Orbis Books, [2023] | Summary: "Henri Nouwen's account of two pilgrimages to Ukraine in the early 1990s, with an introduction by Archbishop Borys Gudziak, setting this story in the context of the current war in Ukraine."— Provided by publisher.
Identifiers: LCCN 2022044645 (print) | LCCN 2022044646 (ebook) | ISBN 9781626985179 (trade paperback) | ISBN 9781608339792 (epub)
Subjects: LCSH: Nouwen, Henri J. M.—Diaries. | Nouwen, Henri J. M.—Travel—Ukraine. | Ukraine—Description and travel.
Classification: LCC BX4705.N87 A3 2023 (print) | LCC BX4705.N87 (ebook) | DDC 282.092 [B]—dc23/eng/20221118
LC record available at https://lccn.loc.gov/2022044645
LC ebook record available at https://lccn.loc.gov/2022044646

Contents

Preface

The publication of this diary by Henri Nouwen, thirty years after it was originally written, calls for some explanation. The fact that Ukraine is currently a focus of global attention might be reason enough to resurrect these long-ago reflections. Yet there is more to this book than its topical relevance. In writing this diary of his travels to Ukraine in 1993 and 1994, Henri was in effect sending a letter to the future. In a mysterious way, it is as if this simple story was waiting for the right time, and for an audience who could appreciate it. And a publisher.

I was not that publisher in 1993 when Henri first approached me about publishing the diary of his trip to Ukraine that summer. He wondered whether I saw the possibility for a book. I did not. Henri, at that time, was one of the most popular spiritual writers in the world, and I had little doubt that anything he published would find an audience. And yet I felt I owed him my honest opinion. Clearly, this eleven-day trip to Ukraine held special meaning for him, but it was not clear what it would mean for other readers. Was it even clear to him? Ukraine was going through the difficult growing pains of independence from the Soviet Union, but it was hardly a subject of wide attention in the United

States. I advised Henri to publish it as a series of articles, and he accepted this idea. His initial diary appeared as a two-part serial in *The New Oxford Review.*

As far as I knew, that was the end of the story. I did not know that this first trip was followed by a second trip to Ukraine in 1994 (also recorded in a diary), nor that at the time of his sudden death in 1996, he was planning further trips to deepen his relationship with the people of Ukraine. Evidently, this was no passing interest. Seeds were being planted for a harvest he would never see. And yet, over the years, those seeds would bear abundant fruit.

Like many things in Henri's life, the original impulse for his trips to Ukraine were rooted in friendship—in this case, a persistent invitation from two special friends. The first of these was Borys Gudziak, whom Henri met while teaching at Harvard Divinity School. Borys, the son of Ukrainian immigrants, was at the time a graduate student in Slavic and Byzantine Cultural Studies at Harvard. Their friendship continued after Henri left Harvard and moved to Toronto to become chaplain for the L'Arche Daybreak Community, while Borys moved to Lviv, Ukraine, and went on to help establish the first Catholic University in the former Soviet Union. (Later he would be ordained as a priest.) The second friend was Zenia Kushpeta, a Canadian, also the child of Ukrainian émigrés, whom Henri had met at Daybreak in his early years there. After independence, she too had decided to move to Ukraine to bring the spirit of L'Arche to her work with handicapped adults there.

I never spoke with Henri about Ukraine again, and had no sense of how deeply these relationships and brief trips had affected him. The next time I thought of Henri's "diary" was in February 2022 when Russia launched a full-scale invasion of Ukraine. Suddenly, everyone in the world was transfixed by the massive sufferings of the Ukrainian people and their brave resistance against seemingly overwhelming odds. I wondered if I could find Henri's original articles online. Instead, I was astonished to discover that a volume of Henri's Ukraine diaries had been translated into Ukrainian just months before. Lo and behold, there was a picture of Borys Gudziak, now an archbishop in the Ukrainian Greek Catholic Church, presenting a copy of Henri's book to the now world-famous President Volodymyr Zelensky!

Soon after, following a fortuitous meeting with Archbishop Gudziak and his assistant Mariana Karapinka, and with the encouragement of the Henri Nouwen Legacy Trust, we conceived the plan of publishing, at long last, an English edition of Henri's book. At first, I agreed to this project more as an opportunity to add to Henri Nouwen's extensive posthumous opus with a work of renewed relevance. But as I read Henri's diaries, especially in light of the two bookends to this edition—the extraordinary introduction by Archbishop Borys and the equally moving afterword by Henri's brother, Laurent Nouwen—I began to realize that there was much more to this simple book than I had originally perceived. With extraordinary prescience, Henri had identified in Ukraine certain spiritual and moral qualities struggling to assert themselves—exactly the qualities, almost thirty years later, that the

Ukrainian people have mobilized in their struggle for freedom and independence. Following their long history of suffering and oppression, he responded in the Ukrainian people to a deep hunger for hope and healing, a need for the life-giving message that he most wanted to share: that we are all "beloved of God," and that God's love seeks out the places where we are most hurt, weak, and vulnerable.

These were themes Henri was especially developing in his last years. This was the particular focus of *Adam: God's Beloved,* about the spiritual lessons he had learned in his early years at Daybreak from the relationship he had formed with Adam, a severely handicapped young man in the community. This was the lesson he most wished to share with the world. And, as it turned out, it would be his final lesson. He suddenly died of a heart attack, while passing through Amsterdam, shortly before his 65th birthday, and only weeks after handing me the manuscript. As Laurent insightfully observes, there was a connection between his response to Adam and his attraction to Ukraine—the marginalized "foster child" of a country within the family of Europe: poor, weak, vulnerable, and yet a vessel of God's love, entrusted with a message and a mission for the wider world.

Archbishop Borys, in his introduction, relates the fruit that this relationship bore in his own life, in the mission of the University, and in contributing to the strength, courage, and spiritual vitality of Ukraine—qualities that have so won the attention and admiration of the world in its most recent, desperate hour.

At the same time, Laurent's afterword describes the incredible fruit of Henri's pilgrimages to Ukraine in providing him, over the last twenty-five years, with a second vocation. Inspired, after Henri's death, by reading his brother's Ukraine diary, Laurent undertook an ongoing mission of solidarity and friendship with Ukraine, delivering over a hundred truckloads of materials and supplies of every kind. At the same time, through the Henri Nouwen Foundation, he has helped support young people in Ukraine in projects to promote social justice, solidarity, and human dignity. And so, following Henri's death, others stepped forward to nurture the seeds planted in these early trips.

No doubt, if he had lived, Henri would have continued to add to this "Ukraine Diary." As it is, the story of his pilgrimage from thirty years ago stands as a kind of time capsule, a window on the time when it was written, which at the same time bears a message for our own time. It is, aside from its universal themes of hope, gratitude, and the power of friendship, also a message directed to all who cherish Henri's memory: that we might carry on and extend his relationship with a proud and long-suffering people he had come to love.

Robert Ellsberg
Publisher, Orbis Books

Introduction

Archbishop Borys Gudziak

Metropolitan Archbishop of Philadelphia
for Ukrainian Catholics in the United States

Head, Department of External Church Relations,
Ukrainian Greek Catholic Church

President, Ukrainian Catholic University, Lviv

Abductions, rockets and artillery fire, waves of refugees, torture and territorial annexation, death and destruction. Ukrainians have been enduring war for almost a decade. But only after February 24, 2022, the onset of Vladimir Putin's full-fledged invasion, did the world focus on the Russian acts of barbarism and genocide in Ukraine—and the broader menace for the international community. Decades after his death, these contemporary calamities mirror the childhood experience of Henri Nouwen in the Netherlands under the Nazis during World War II. Thirty years ago, he had an ominous sense that something reflecting the horrors of his youth could return. The age of imperialism was not over. Independent Ukraine was just emerging from the euphoria of newfound freedom. A sensitive man ever yearning for God's peace and love, Henri Nouwen had premonitions of violence and war. He was not naïve.

Father Henri Nouwen—professor at Notre Dame, Yale, and Harvard, pastor in the L'Arche Daybreak Community, author of some fifty books and intercontinental lecturer—was himself a pilgrim to many lands on different continents. Henri sought to discern how God works in history and in the lives of human beings in whatever land they may inhabit. The Dutchman who spent most of his adulthood in the United States and Canada was an explorer, pioneer, innovator, and impresario of communication regarding life in the Holy Spirit. This he did personally—engaging patiently and loyally with those who came or wrote to him, locally—creating and fostering community, and globally—ceaselessly searching for new meaning and intimacy with God and sharing it with a vast readership.

Henri scrutinized how life with God is lived in different cultures. Each new country and context served as a mirror to reflect on his own journey with Jesus in order to offer inspiring insight for his audiences and readers. In his last years, Henri had two secretaries to help handle letters from his correspondents, to whom he was most faithful, and to respond to the one hundred speaking invitations that he received every week. Henri was a busy man, frenetically so, with a packed agenda. And so, it may surprise some of his readers that in his last few years, Ukraine became for Henri Nouwen an important place of reference, a spiritual *locus*. In fact, as recorded in the *Sabbatical Journey,* a diary of his last year, he made a commitment to come to Ukraine for a semester to write, preach, and teach at the Lviv Theological Academy, today the Ukrainian Catholic University (UCU). Alas, he died suddenly a few weeks later.

The country that Henri explored in the mid-1990s is now being discovered by a global community, itself facing searing questions of the soul. Distant, arcane geography becomes vivid, even lurid. Not only Kyiv and Lviv, but also the killing fields of Bucha, Borodianka, Irpin, and Izium today are household names. After "Never again!" how could this be happening in the twenty-first century? Mariupol, the besieged and leveled city of Mary, became a prayer of millions. In the hyperbolic words of *New York Times*' Thomas Friedman, it may be "the first true *world war*,—much more than World War I or World War II ever was. In this ... World War Wired, virtually everyone on the planet can either observe the fighting at a granular level, participate in some way or be affected economically—no matter where they live." Millions of posts, photos, videos, and direct streaming bring unprecedented sustained transnational attention to a poor, humbled country's valiant resistance against a resurgent wannabe empire. Henri visited the nation of Ukraine in its nativity. Now, in the minds of many, it is being born again. This advent, marked by pain and blood, is transforming the world.

Tormented yet intrepid, Ukraine is at the epicenter of global change. International political and military alliances, the world's economy and energy strategies, agriculture, food policy, and ecology are all being reformatted by the Russian invasion of the country. Ukrainian resilience has forged unity in the European community, which after Brexit had been experiencing uncertainty and geographical fissures. NATO has a new sense of purpose, with the imminent inclusion of two new member states, Finland and Sweden. Russia's partners in the

BRICS community (Brazil, India, China, and South Africa) seem to be reconsidering the nature of their alliances with the aggressor nation. With deliveries blocked from the "Breadbasket of Europe," millions in the Near East and Africa face food shortages and famine. Global inflation, provoked significantly by higher energy prices, is further crippling the poor on all continents. For many, winter became colder and darker. The specter of nuclear war has arisen like never before in the past two generations.

The Russian invasion and Ukrainian resistance to it are provoking a global upheaval. All three—the invasion, resistance, and upheaval—have caught the world by surprise, completely unprepared. A quick Putin victory would have further undermined a rules-based international order and been a boon to authoritarian rulers in China and North Korea, Vietnam and Belarus. Russia's neo-imperial stature would have enhanced its influence exerted through authoritarian states like Venezuela, Cuba, Syria, and Iran. If Ukraine had collapsed in the predicted three or seven days or even months, the political and social displacements would have been only regional, or so it was thought. The invasion and expected conquest would have been lost among the twenty-odd simmering or hot military conflicts waged on the planet. An annihilated Ukraine would have been obscured in the grand East–West symmetries, the polar balancing between global powers: an object, a pitied victim, a puppet. *Realpolitik* would have prevailed, the approach in which the agendas of the superpowers are all that really matter and the little ones of the world can be crushed by the giants, subjugated by empires, marginalized and forgotten.

Might makes right. Principles and human beings are sidelined, God's truth about who we are, the dignity of every person— expediently relegated.

But Ukrainians resist. Bravely, selflessly. Solidarity, prayer, mutual trust, volunteer work and community charity, sacrifice, faith, and a belief in eternity all are present in a new way in society. People are certain that the truth will prevail and that evil will be defeated. There is a shared moral inspiration. No one is giving up or is ready to compromise the defense of God-given human dignity. In the face of Putin's expressed genocidal intent and his army's war crimes, convictions are clarified as is belief in ethical objectivity: some things are unambiguously true, and others are patently false; there is distinct good and there is absolute evil. For these convictions, tens of thousands have given their lives. Knowing full well the brutal dangers and mortal risks, hundreds of thousands of men and women—the Ukrainian armed forces are 20 percent female—have volunteered and continue to enlist for the defense of family, friends and neighbors, innocent civilians, homes and businesses, cities and villages.

A normal, self-preserving and self-serving rationale cannot explain such a reaction. It goes against the logic of the natural realm. There is something supernatural, even Christ-like, in this sacrificial love. Jesus said: "No one has greater love than this, to lay down one's life for one's friends" (Jn. 15:13). This reaction and self-offering of Ukrainians is mesmerizing the world. The defenders do not want anything that rightfully belongs to the Russians. They want only their own freedom and dignity, refusing to be owned and objectified. Henri prayed for the healing of the traumas of the past, recognizing the victimization of Ukrainians that went on for centuries. He saw symbols of valor in the face of oppression when he met the living martyrs who emerged from the outlawed catacomb Church of the Soviet times, viciously suppressed by Moscow for two generations. The capacity to witness radically has returned. Did he foresee this happening?

The Russians mercilessly pummel apartment buildings, domestic dwellings, energy grids, hospitals and schools, churches, museums, and the very neighborhoods that Henri visited in 1993 and 1994. Cruise missiles zoom over the summer camp sites where Henri led retreats. When the aggressors falter and fail on the eastern military fronts, they assail the civilian infrastructure throughout the country, inflicting misery upon tens of millions. President Putin threatens nuclear attack to terrorize and dispirit the entire population and cow the international community. Yet the fear of the victims has been replaced by righteous anger and resolute resistance. Miraculously, David stands up to Goliath. The Russians' brutality galvanizes widespread global solidarity with the victims. The world comes to know Ukraine as Ukrainians come to recognize themselves. Is this what Henri expected?

It would have been fascinating to listen to or read Henri's spiritual discernment of these contemporary developments, both the tragedy and the heroism. He was an astute cultural and social witness to the plight of the vulnerable, an incisive assessor of human character and behavior in both its strengths and weaknesses. In our conversations in the years before his death, Henri was bemused by an increasingly prevailing global cult of comfort. An enthusiast of reform and renewal, always open to novelty and growth, he could not but be disconcerted by the wholesale deconstruction of just about everything, including much that is lifegiving in the Christian tradition. He would have appreciated people taking a stand, risking their lives for God-given principles and values, for the weak and innocent, doing so in a transactional age when most things can be bought and sold, when there is an increasing dictatorship of relativism in a domain of post-truth propaganda and politics, ethics and epistemology, in a world that doubts that truth is possible and increasingly finds it difficult to encounter Him who is the Truth (Jn. 14:16).

How would Henri Nouwen speak on matters of war, peace, and justice in this context? How would he react to the war crimes, to the imminent, in fact incipient, and clearly intentional genocide? What would he try to do for the 14 million people who have been displaced from their homes, who have lost their possession, livelihood, and loved ones? Henri suffered much personal anguish. Some of the main themes of his writings, in which he openly shares his sense of failure, rejection, loss, loneliness, and abandonment, focus on the struggle to recognize and accept God's abiding presence, generosity, fidelity, and love. How would he convey to the homeless that they are welcome in the House of the Father? How would the author of the *Wounded Healer* console and grieve with and for the hundreds of thousands who have been injured, maimed, or killed? Henri led many to *Behold the Beauty of the Lord* by introducing them to the practice of *Praying with Icons.* He used Russian icons for his meditations. How would he assess the Russian Orthodox Church's active support for the war and theologically contorted apology for what amounts to genocide? How would the author of *The Life of the Beloved* express God's love and mercy? *Making All Things New* is something Henri wrote about; what counsel would he give for the effort to rebuild?

Had he been still alive and able, I am sure Henri Nouwen would have again come to Ukraine—this time with his brother Laurent—and would have written another segment of the book in your hands. He would have shared his experiences of prayer and communion with God amid the destruction and despair. Henri would not have avoided the difficult questions; he would have delved into the suffering. He would have offered inspiration as he did in so many circumstances. He would have taken moral initiative. Henri would have led with charity, representing Jesus among the suffering and marginalized. I miss him, his wisdom, words, and ministry at the time of this catastrophe.

*   *   *

The *Ukraine Diary* is not a comprehensive presentation of Ukraine or an analysis of the ongoing war. Yet Henri Nouwen, who died in 1996, has quite a bit to say about the land that has captured the world's imagination. Many readers will be surprised by how he came to understand the issues underlying contemporary events, and how prophetic some of his observations were:

> *We keep wondering whether the future will be any*
> *different. With so many voices in Russia that want to*
> *reclaim Ukraine as part of their territory, there is the*
> *constant fear that independence might be a very fragile*
> *thing. The fact that the United States pays so much atten-*
> *tion to Russia and so little to Ukraine, except in trying*
> *to have it give up its nuclear arsenal, makes Ukrainians*
> *question how much international support their indepen-*
> *dence will get when push comes to shove.*

> *August 1993*

Henri was encountering a country engaged in an unprec-edented process to enhance peace on Earth. No country before or since has done it. Ukraine, along with Belarus and Kazakh-stan, was negotiating with the United States, United Kingdom, and Russia to unilaterally give up its nuclear arsenal, the third biggest on the planet. Its nuclear stockpile was larger than those of France, the United Kingdom, and China combined. For many, nuclear disarmament is a dream. And here it happened! And yet this prophetic step and the promises made have all but been forgotten, left unappreciated, even by peace activists. As Henri feared, Ukraine's vulnerability would be exploited.

On the basis of the Budapest Memorandum, signed on December 5, 1994, Russia, Britain and the U.S. pledged to guarantee Ukraine's sovereignty and territorial integrity and to refrain from threatening or using force against Ukraine. They vowed not to use nuclear arms against the signatories. The three powers promised not to utilize economically coer-cive methods to undermine Ukraine's sovereignty and to seek

United Nations Security Council action should Ukraine be threatened by nuclear weapons. Between 1991 and 2014 Ukraine reduced its 900,000-soldier military force by some 80 percent. The leadership and population of the country were not interested in any transnational aggression, much less anti-Russian. The hope was for peace, economic prosperity, democracy, and a free and vibrant civil society. Early on, Henri saw that there were clouds hanging over these hopes. The Russian invasion and nuclear saber-rattling reveal how prescient were his geo-political intuitions.

> *What struck me most was that independence is a new concept for Ukraine. Except for the two years of failed independence in the post-World War I years, Ukraine has in modern times never experienced a clear national identity. Even today there are many discussions about the nature of the Ukrainian state. Is it a political, an ethnic or a territorial unity? Is there enough basis on which to build a state? Many Russians consider present-day Ukraine a totally artificial entity. Is there enough inner cohesion to keep together a nation that has little experience of statehood and which includes a 25 percent minority population? Or is it doomed to be torn apart constantly by inner strife and outer aggression? At present there is a lot of anxiety around these questions.*

> *August 1994*

These were the early years of Ukrainian independence, and Putin was just an ambitious lackey carrying the briefcase of the mayor of St. Petersburg, but even back then Henri, ever the attentive observer and keen listener, was able to sense how fragile was the peace, how vulnerable was Ukraine.

These two quotes, which identify the danger of Russian neocolonialism, reveal the author's sense of the situation and comprehension of the country in which he spent only a couple of weeks. Those who knew Henri Nouwen in life or are acquainted with him through his books know a priest of broad mindset and surprisingly diverse interests and uncanny sensibilities.

Whether it was the fathers and mothers of the Egyptian desert of the first centuries of Christianity, or contemporary prophets such as Dorothy Day and Thomas Merton, the Gospel-driven movements for social and racial justice in the United States or Latin America, the ivory tower of Ivy league universities, people with intellectual disabilities, or circus actors—the people and places that Henri encountered and wrote about present a broad spectrum of humanity. In all instances, Henri honed in on the human spiritual condition: who is Jesus for the concrete people in each context, what is God communicating to them and through them to us, and how.

For almost four decades Henri was on the move. The titles of his books reflect his itinerant mind and soul: *The Genesee Diary, Clowning in Rome, Love in a Fearful Land: A Guatemalan Story*, and *The Road to Daybreak*. A readership of millions in more than thirty languages, representing different cultures, found sustenance for the soul from what Henri had to say through his own soul journey. He speaks to us today in Finnish and Korean, Portuguese and Indonesian, Polish and

Ukrainian. Henri took the time to explore cultures and learn languages. He could preach not only in Dutch and English but also in Spanish, French, and German. Many people reading Henri's straightforward and simple words discover the cultural depth that stands behind his search to articulate the message of God's love. He was fundamentally interested in the relationship between God and the human person. His intellectual pursuits and international travels brought him into contact with very different expressions of the Christian life. His unique talent to go to the core of God's relationship with people in the Ukrainian context, as he did in others, is the main merit of this book.

* * *

As a seminarian in Rome in the spring of 1983, I read one of Henri's books; I cannot remember which one it was, because eventually I read them almost all. On the back cover, his Yale affiliation was identified. Since I was coming back to the United States and going to Harvard in the fall, the thought crossed my mind: "Wouldn't it be great if there was somebody like that 'Newwen' guy—as I erroneously pronounced it— teaching at the rival university?" What a surprise when after my first semester immersed in Slavic studies, I discovered in a course catalog of the Divinity School that Professor Henri Nouwen now lectures at my new alma mater.

Our encounter in the context of his teaching at Harvard Divinity School (HDS) in the spring semester of 1984 initi- ated a gentle trajectory that would eventually bring Henri to another marginal place: post-Soviet Ukraine. I signed up for

Henri's "Introduction to Spirituality" course along with some three hundred students. Many of his readers consider Henri's writings to be among the most influential Christian texts of the latter part of the twentieth century. Yet his public speaking, lecturing, and preaching, in my opinion, were even more powerful and compelling. They have had a seminal influence on my life and ministry. I had the privilege to listen hundreds of times. Those who have not would do well to view the few videos available on the internet to get a sense of the passionate, personal, prophetic Henri Nouwen.

We had a first conversation, after one of the first lectures of the semester, in February 1984. Henri was a world-renowned religious author and authority. I was a rather unsure 23-year-old student enduring a bit of culture shock at postmodern and plush Harvard to which I had arrived after living and studying in Rome at the traditional and austere seminary of Patriarch Josyf Slipyj, a man who had endured eighteen years of the Gulag. By character and disposition Father Nouwen and Cardinal Slipyj were polar opposites. But they shared a common commitment to God and God's people. I had left Rome with the Patriarch's blessing, hoping to encounter someone like "Newwen." I was no longer in a strict house of formation where one's day was regimented from 5:30 a.m. to 10:00 p.m. My new spiritual and intellectual quest seemed for some of my superiors and friends to be a deviation from the path to ministry. For many years I pursued historical and philological studies, but I never abandoned the call to the priesthood. On the contrary, I believed that my graduate studies in Slavic and Byzantine cultural and church history would help me live and develop my priestly vocation. Henri would become a guide on this route.

The possibility of cross-registration, which was a privilege for students at theological schools in Boston, meant that hundreds of students from outside Harvard clamored to come to Henri Nouwen's courses. Few were disappointed. For many, the course was life-changing. Yet, not all at HDS were pleased. In fact, Henri himself left Harvard after only two semesters of teaching. A contingent of ideologically disposed students and faculty considered Henri not sufficiently enthusiastic about certain contemporary issues. Indeed, Henri was interested in authentic experience with God, not ideology. Most of all, Henri was craving real Christian community, something that he preached about, but something that elite academic institutions do not necessarily foster. The Lord would keep Henri on the move.

Henri's classes fascinated me by the depth and simplicity of his presentation: he prayed and pondered intensely, yet wrote and spoke simply and accessibly, focusing on the essence of the spiritual, which was not a negation of the material realm. Quite the opposite: his approach and language were sacramental, artistic, symbolic. He was a charismatic and effective communicator of life in Christ. He himself delved deeply into different aspects of the relationship between a loving God and the wounded person. Jesus was his friend, teacher, and guide. We followed along.

Henri was constantly looking for the most effective words and categories to share this experience. He made Jesus near and intimate. The nature and quality of one's relationship with God was at the core of his ministry, sermons, and books. I remember when, as if thinking aloud, Henri analyzed how others write on religious and psychological topics, trying to learn from them. He strove to write and preach in a user-friendly way, to be as close as possible to people. His priority was to connect, to be in communion, and therefore to live simply and sincerely, with attention to the God-given dignity of each person, without wasting time and effort on fruitless ideological dialectics or battles. As his friends and readers know, this did not always come easily for Henri.

His rousing words were mixed with a light sense of humor, often self-deprecating. Henri knew how to laugh at himself … most of the time. He constantly searched for the path from loneliness to solitude with God, from alienation to communion with others, and from feeling lost to returning to the Father's House. I was impressed by Henri's general erudition and knowledge of history, the development of church doctrine, and art. Yet his learning was not dryly encyclopedic. He was not in pursuit of omniscience. General learnedness was important to Henri because it helped him understand the essence and modalities of life in Christ embracing the human experience in its entirety. He was genuinely interested in people and cultures, not mere historical facts and abstract arguments. His *Ukraine Diary* reflects this predilection.

We met as professor and student, got to know each other as guide and one looking for guidance. Over time our interaction grew into a real friendship. Henri most profoundly touched me in a context of domestic, community prayer. A small room in the so-called "Carriage House" where Henri lived near HDS served as his home chapel. He invited me to join the prayer circle he led. For a semester I participated in a tranquil dawn routine of liturgy and meditation. There were no more than a dozen of us. We did not talk much. All the participants arrived just before the start of prayer at 7:30. After the Morning Office, a half hour of silence, and the Eucharist with Henri's homily we quickly, without chatter, dispersed for 9:00 a.m. lectures or other responsibilities. In this contemplative, sacramental atmosphere, mostly without conversation, our relationship grew. At the end to the semester, I invited Henri to come to a concert of Ukrainian liturgical and folk music presented by the Christ the King Ukrainian Catholic Church Choir from Jamaica Plains at the Swedenborgian Church on Harvard's campus. Henri came to hear us sing. For me it was a great honor and joy. For Henri it was probably the first encounter with Ukrainian culture.

After Harvard, Henri spent a sabbatical year in France getting to know the L'Arche movement. He invited me to visit him, which I did. After he moved to Toronto to the Daybreak L'Arche community, I was a regular guest of Henri's. Despite the distance, our friendship developed. Henri's help was crucial in difficult moments, both personal and academic. His advice about the discipline of writing helped me get back on track with my dissertation. I finally finished it before moving to Lviv in the summer of 1992 to work on the project of developing the Ukrainian Catholic University.

*   *   *

In 1993 and 1994, Zenia Kushpeta, the founder of Faith and Light and L'Arche in Ukraine, and I invited Henri to Lviv. We were eager to share with him and other friends from L'Arche, who figure prominently in the *Ukraine Diary*, our world, one traumatized by totalitarianism but one full of hope and determination to rebuild. I also wanted the Church in Ukraine and the future university team to be inspired by Henri's insightful perspectives on living a life in Christ. Henri became directly involved in forming the vision of the university, which came to place ostracized persons with different mental abilities at the center of its identity. We needed the help and witness of the so-called "disabled" to address the post-traumatic shock, i.e., the post-totalitarian disabilities of Ukrainians shared with some two billion people between Estonia and Albania and China and Vietnam that endured communist rule or continue to do so.

As Henri was keen to learn and record in the *Ukraine Diary*, in the twentieth century some fifteen million persons in Ukraine were killed or died an unnatural death as a result of world wars and genocidal regimes, both Soviet and Nazi. The enduring system of political, social, cultural, and religious repression weighed heavily on every citizen. If over three generations a system kills systematically, every member of society naturally develops a reflex of protection not only against the system, but against "the other," since the other is potentially dangerous. In Ukraine, and in all post-Soviet lands, this fear entered deeply into the psychological and spiritual DNA of the population. Trust—the basic prerequisite for interpersonal relations, family life, civic activity, social communication, business, politics—was profoundly undermined and needed to be systematically, gently, and lovingly restored. A profound healing process through the touch, word, presence, and communion with Christ the healer was a central calling and mandate of the Church and its educational institutions.

Inspired by the world of L'Arche, brought to Ukraine by Zenia, Henri, and other members of the Daybreak Community, a decision was made at the very beginning to invite people with special needs into the life of the nascent Ukrainian Catholic University (UCU), so that they could act as tutors of human relations, as teachers who would help us see God in each other. Our friends with different mental abilities do not care if one has high SAT scores, is rich or powerful, a winner in competitions, glamorous or famous. They care about and express one fundamental truth of the Gospel, asking with their presence and being Jesus's most basic question: "Do you love me?" This is what our Lord asks Peter and the apostles. This is what he asks each of us. It is the most important pedagogical question. Under Henri's influence UCU placed this question at the heart of the university's identity.

The university assumed the challenge to revive and foster trust, both in God and one's neighbor. UCU is an intellectually ambitious institution, which today has the highest average incoming student SAT scores in the country and ten applicants for every opening in many programs. And yet with the influence of Henri Nouwen, a theological decision was taken: to invite into the heart of a competitive academic community those that will mitigate zero sum competitive achievement attitudes: people without academic ambition, persons with different mental ability. Today, during the devastating Russian invasion, when trauma is being multiplied and the need for personal and societal healing grows exponentially, this gentle spirituality and theology of life takes on particularly powerful meaning. UCU has served as haven of humanitarian relief and housing and a coordinating center for civic solidarity. Many members of the university are on the front lines. Sadly, many have been killed. Studies have continued, but the most important "courses" and "seminars" have been the lessons of the war, which clarify many Gospel truths and call all members of the community to a deeper understanding and practice of charity, courage, generosity—a very practical love of one's neighbor.

* * *

Henri traveled to Ukraine twice. Not as a tourist and not out of simple curiosity, but as a pilgrim and a missionary of healing. Like almost all Western Europeans in the 1990s, before the trips he knew little about Ukraine and the identity of its people. That was a time when for most, even highly educated people from outside the Slavic realm, Ukraine was indistinguishable from Russia. For example, a Ukrainian athlete competing for the Soviet Olympic team was called a Russian, as was a Moldovan, Armenian, Kazakh, or Azeri athlete. In Western popular culture, the "mystical otherness" of Russian culture and the unquestionable permanence of a "Russian Empire" were generally not subjected to critical analysis. The eleven time zones of the Soviet Union were "Russia," and the histories of some 190 nations and ethnic groups subjected to a colonial empire were non-distinct, not identifiable, and not understood.

The myth of "Holy Russia" (would one ever say "Holy Spain," "Holy Poland," or "Holy Brazil"?) with her icons and imposing liturgy, the image of a Russian imperial culture represented by Tolstoy and Dostoyevsky, the Kirov Ballet, Tchaikovsky and Mussorgsky fascinated and enticed long after the imperialist legacy of Austria-Hungary and the Ottomans, Spain and Portugal, Belgium and Germany, France and Great Britain endured withering social and moral critique. The European colonial empires underwent de-colonization and political dismemberment but the notion of Russian empire endured, remaining somehow "natural," acceptable. Even though global social justice movements formulated compelling condemnation of all forms of colonialism, the idea that Russia can have dominion over the lands and cultures of tens of millions of people who belong to subject nations and ethnic groups did not cause reflexive scandal. It still doesn't with proponents of *Realpolitik*.

Henri's introduction to Ukraine came at a time when post-Soviet freedom was fresh and fragile, but clearly desired. In December 1991, 92 percent of Ukrainians had voted for independence from the Soviet Union and liberty from Russian domination. The Russian invasion, war crimes, and genocidal acts are only confirming this conviction. Ukrainians will not return to imperial subject status: If Americans do not ever see themselves as being subjects of Britain, if Brazil will never again be a colony of Portugal, Argentina or Uruguay of Spain, Algeria or Morocco of France, if Blacks will never be slaves of Whites, Ukrainians today are saying "we will never again be colonial subjects of the Russians." These were the sentiments behind the posture of people that Henri met in Lviv in the 1990s. Today, they are articulated through a resistance by the whole nation paying the highest price.

The discriminating reader will notice that Henri was not completely free of the myth of a Great Russia. But he was far ahead of most because he listened attentively to his hosts. His authentic curiosity about human experience and the desire to look at new circumstances with the eyes of love gave Henri a unique capacity to get to know Ukraine and Ukrainians as subjects even when their self-awareness was in a process of growth.

Readers of the modest *Ukraine Diary* that Henri wrote during his two brief but intense visits will discover how considerate the author was to the people and the reality of a downtrodden and objectified populace and place. Attentive and discerning. To this day many remember Henri and his visits warmly and vividly. Pictures with Henri from the retreats and celebrations are on the mantles of those that participated. Henri deeply touched the wounds of the country and the culture by meeting and embracing concrete people, especially those who were broken in a browbeaten land.

Our trips to Ukraine show us another type of handicap.
It is the handicap that comes from a broken history, from
centuries of oppression and exploitation, from neglect
and indifference of the wealthy nations, from the social
sins of injustice and greed. Not only people with mental
handicaps are marginalized in our world, but countries
as well. Ukraine is one of the marginalized countries
among the international community of nations. Men
and women with mental handicaps in Ukraine are the
marginalized people in a marginalized country.

August 1994

In this book, the reader will not find a comprehensive analysis of political, social, and cultural developments but rather a heart-to-heart encounter of suffering people with a gentle, rapt observer who was ready to listen carefully to their stories. Henri listened and spoke about Jesus, described the Father's love, and shared the gifts of the Holy Spirit. Some, perhaps for the first time, felt truly listened to and heard out. For some, the words of the Gospel came alive for the first time. The tall English-speaking Dutch priest with dynamic hand gestures and large eyes was interested in the story the little ones had to tell. It was the story of God's little ones, and Henri would tell it to others, now a quarter century after his death.

This modest, seemingly simple book about a visit to a distant land is in fact a subtle tale of how encounter genuinely and radically changes the lives of people. I can testify that much of what has happened in my life is the fruit of the seed that the Lord planted in my heart through Henri Nouwen. The Ukrainian Catholic University's identity and style are under the clear influence of Henri's witness and message. Those compassion-filled days in 1993 and 1994 gave impetus to the Faith and Light and L'Arche movements in Ukraine, to numerous youth initiatives, and to a university that is a model for educational reform in the country and in the forefront of social, cultural, and moral transformation.

There has been dramatic change in the past three decades in Ukraine. The present resilience in the face of brutal invasion is one stage in Ukraine's ongoing pilgrimage from fear to dignity. Ukrainians are freeing themselves of post-totalitarian trauma and complexes, claiming their God-given worth, and discovering their identity as people beloved by the Lord. Henri would have appreciated the transfiguration occurring, one in which Jesus is leading his people on a way of the Cross to a new life.

After Henri's death, his brother Laurent Nouwen inherited Henri's commitment to this seemingly forsaken land. Henri's writing, especially the *Ukraine Diary*, motivated Laurent to serve the poor and marginalized in Ukraine, which he has done in an extraordinary and most humble manner.

Thanks to Laurent, his brother's manuscript received new life. Its publication after so many years reveals an aspect of Henri Nouwen that has remained largely unknown. It also gives deeper understanding of the country which in 2022 has emerged from the margins and become an epicenter of global transformation, finding itself in the heart of history and the heart of God.

PART ONE

July 24–August 14, 1993

Rotterdam—Saturday, July 24, 1993

Today I have decided to start a Ukrainian diary. On August 1 I will go to Ukraine for an eleven-day visit. Although my departure is still eight days away I am aware that this diary needs a substantial introduction, so that this rather short trip may be something more than an interesting or eye-opening excursion. I really want it to be an occasion for some form of conversion.

This may sound pretentious, but as the date of my departure approaches, I feel an increasing inner tension. Some voice within me says, "You have to make a choice. This can be just one more educational experience or it can be a chance to be touched in a vital, new way. But it is your choice." This inner voice finally drew me to the library in Rotterdam, where I am currently spending time with my brother and his family. I needed to find a quiet corner and ask myself, *What am I hoping for?*

I know very little about Ukraine and would never have chosen to go there were it not for two close friends living there: Zenia Kushpeta and Borys Gudziak. Zenia is a member of the L'Arche Daybreak community in Toronto, where I have been living these last seven years, and Borys is a graduate in Slavic studies, whom I came to know during my years at Harvard Divinity School. I am really going because of them. Otherwise, Ukraine seems so full of tension and conflict that it evokes more fear in me than attraction. But Zenia and Borys kept pleading, "You must come!" Their "musts" conveyed a genuine urgency— almost like a "spiritual must"—that made me feel I truly *must* go, because there, where I least expect it, something may be waiting to touch me deeply and lead me to a completely new place.

But there is more to say about the reason for this journey. Zenia's and Borys's "musts" emerge from their own stories, and I have to tell these stories first so as to be able to write my own. Borys and I met when I was teaching pastoral theology at Harvard Divinity School, and he was finishing his doctoral work in Slavic studies. We often had occasion to get together, at first as professor and student, then as priest and penitent, then as counselor and seeker for directions, and finally as friends. (Now the roles are often reversed, though today we are first and foremost friends.)

Borys gives the impression of a very quiet and deliberate person. I would often try to fire him up, to show excitement about what he was doing, to inspire him to new and greater things. But as the years went by, I discovered that he had no lack of passion, especially when it came to giving his life to others, his deep determination to complete the tasks he had begun, his stubbornness, and—yes, beneath his quiet demeanor—a true charismatic fervor and commitment to faithful friendship.

I still remember the moment—more than eight years ago—when we sat across from each other at the large table in my study. Borys wanted to speak about his vocation: "What does God want of me?" he asked. "I was in Rome at the Ukrainian Seminary. I came to Harvard for Slavic studies. I desire to be close to God … but still … am I called to become a priest, to work in Ukraine, to teach, to get married, to have a family?"

With a conviction that took me by surprise, I said to him, "I know that God has a very special role for you. Stay close to God's heart and let God guide you. You will know what you are called to do when you have to know it."

In the years that followed, Borys visited Ukraine regularly. After Ukrainian independence, he was one of the main organizers of a large youth rally of the Ukrainian Greek Catholic Church. [The "Ukranian Youth for Christ" rally was held September 7-8, 1990.] Meanwhile, he finished his dissertation and moved to Ukraine to collect the oral history of the underground Greco-Catholic Church since its suppression in 1946 and to explore further his own vocation. After I had moved from the Harvard Divinity School in Cambridge, Massachusetts, to the L'Arche Daybreak community in Toronto—where I now share my life with people with mental handicaps—Borys came often to visit me there. During these visits he began to urge me to come to Ukraine.

Still, I kept hesitating. Yes, I wanted to go, but there were so many other things to do! Finally, it wasn't Borys but Zenia who compelled me to step over my excuses and made me pin down dates: August 1–11, 1993.

I met Zenia soon after coming to L'Arche Daybreak in August 1986. Zenia had lived at Daybreak for a year, 1984–1985. During my first year there, she continued to visit the community every week. She is one of the most energetic, spirited people I have ever met. She speaks as if everyone and everything is full of light, beauty, and truth. I remember the time she explained why she always came to our house on Wednesday evenings. "Henri, I can't cook," she said. "I can only make spaghetti and meatballs. That is why I come here on Wednesday night when spaghetti and meatballs are on the menu and I can cook!" Then she added with a smile, "but I obviously come for Rosie too."

Rosie, one of the most handicapped people in our community, was Zenia's favorite person. For Zenia, Rosie was a princess, deserving of every honor: nice clothes, good food, and plenty of attention. Zenia gave it all. One day she even flew with Rosie to New York City to go shopping at Bloomingdale's!

Zenia's special gift is music. She is an accomplished concert pianist, and she would often practice for six hours a day while preparing for recitals and concerts. But something profound happened to her. Her heart was captured by handicapped people. When this became clear, she didn't hesitate to leave her musical career and join Daybreak, no longer as a regular visitor but as a permanent member.

But then Ukraine became independent. For Zenia, that was a watershed experience. Born to parents who had emigrated from Ukraine, and raised with a deep national consciousness, she began to wonder if she shouldn't go to her own country and visit there the many handicapped people who received nothing of the love and care that Rosie received. First it was just an idea, then it became a vision, and finally it grew into a clear decision.

Daybreak advised her first to make a short two-week visit to Ukraine to determine whether a longer stay would be realistic. Many of us thought that the hard and complex situation in her homeland would dampen her excitement a little. But the opposite happened. I still remember the evening when Zenia spoke to the whole community about her two-week visit. The pictures she showed of the handicapped children whom she had met in the orphanage in Lviv were so moving that everyone wanted to support her desire to return and look for ways to offer these children care, affection, and possibly a home.

Zenia had the determination and vision to do something for the forgotten people of Ukraine. But it would be far from easy. The needs were enormous, the facilities very poor, and the bureaucracy in state and church very frustrating.

Zenia soon realized that, unless she could receive solid support from her community in Canada, she would drown in the sea of needs. She needed to be sent by her community—to know that her going to Ukraine was a mission. She needed to know and feel that she could be in Ukraine in the name of Rosie and the other handicapped people she loved so much. In sending many members of Daybreak to Honduras, Mexico, India, and other places, it has become clear to us how important such a mission is. Life far from home can be hard, but when lived as a mission many difficulties can be lived as graces!

During her last visit to Canada her "must" to me was clearer than ever. "You must come and see where I work and live. You must speak to my friends, visit the homes I visit and most of all share the vision of L'Arche with my people. There is such a need, not just a material need, but also, and most of all, a spiritual need. The young people are often so discouraged. They need to know about prayer, community, and care for the poor. They need to get good teaching, especially good inspiration. You *must* come." My protests were loud and clear. "I have never been there; I don't know anything about the people's lives and struggles; I don't speak a word of Ukrainian, and with my deep roots in the Latin Catholic Church, I wonder how welcome I will be in the Catholic Church of the Eastern Rite. On top of it all: what will I be able to do for the handicapped people there?"

But Zenia pushed all my anxieties away: "Just come, just see, just speak, just be yourself. Don't worry about these things. You must come and you know … Borys will also be there!"

And so it all came together. Borys and Zenia would both show me their country, their people, their work, and I would let them guide me even where I rather would not go.

Happily, I am not going alone to Ukraine. Nathan Ball, the director of the Daybreak community, will join me. Nathan also knows Zenia very well and has discussed at length her Ukrainian plans. He is deeply committed to strengthening the bond between the Daybreak community and Zenia's work with the mentally handicapped people in Lviv. Nathan became convinced, not only that it was good for Zenia to have the community's support, but that it was also good for the community to be directly connected with her. The many stories Zenia told made him aware of the privileged positions of mentally handicapped people in Canada when compared with their counterparts in the countries of the former Soviet Union. He has offered her his personal support and the support of the community.

It is a special joy for me that Nathan and I can experience Ukraine together. As director and pastor of the Daybreak community, we can make this visit much more than a visit to give personal support to Zenia and Borys. It is also a mission. We are sent to Ukraine to visit Zenia in the name of the community and to return with ideas and suggestions for the future.

Nathan is a Canadian who just celebrated his fortieth birthday. We met in the L'Arche community in Trosly, France, and came together to Daybreak in August 1986. It would be an understatement to say that we lived a lot together during the last seven years. Our friendship has gone through many hills and valleys. Our work together in the community has been filled with moments of great satisfaction and painful disagreements. We have much in common: love for the gospel of Jesus, love for L'Arche, love for theology, and love for community and ministry. We also are very different, not only in age, but also in character and disposition. But after seven years in the same community, our friendship has grown stronger and deeper, not only despite, but also because of the great pains we have experienced in our relationship. It is the first time we have undertaken a long trip together. I am full of trust that this trip will not simply give each of us much to think about but will also bring our friendship into a new place. With Zenia and Borys as our guides, we will be able to see, hear, and feel things that we would never be able to see, hear, or feel on our own.

It is going to be an adventure in many ways: an adventure in a new world of people, ideas, and aspirations and also an adventure in a new world of inner experiences of faith, trust, and friendship. I have no idea what I will be writing in the days to come, but I am committed to write directly, honestly, and very concretely about these two types of adventures.

⚜

Rotterdam—Sunday, July 25, 1993

Yesterday, Borys called from his parents' home in Syracuse, New York. For the last few weeks he had been in the Ukrainian Catholic Monastery of the Transfiguration, north of San Francisco, to pray and to teach. Each summer he is part of a small faculty—connected with the University of St. Paul in Ottawa—that introduces students to the spirituality of the Christian East through contemplation and study. [These summer schools were organized by the Metropolitan Andrey Sheptytsky Institute of Eastern Christian Studies, which today is an autonomous academic unit of the Faculty of Theology of the University of St. Michael's College in the University of Toronto.] This year he had come especially from Ukraine to teach this unique "summer course."

But, as he told me on the telephone, he is eager to go back to Lviv and continue his work there. His time at the monastery as well as his time with his family had deepened his conviction that Ukraine was where he must be. He is quite excited at the prospect of our being together soon. He is planning to fly to London where Nathan and I will connect with him.

Zenia's plan for our trip is that Nathan and I will give a weekend retreat for the young people in Lviv, spend two evenings with parents of handicapped people, and offer a few workshops here and there. Borys will serve as translator. Meanwhile, I wrote a little booklet for the retreat, which Zenia translated and Nathan printed.

I am very glad that Nathan, Borys, and I will have a few days in England before flying via Warsaw to Lviv. We have been invited to stay with Bart and Patricia Gavigan at their conference center, Brookplace in Chobham, Surrey; this will give us an opportunity to rest and prepare ourselves for the trip.

Chobham—Monday, July 26, 1993

This morning I flew on a KLM Cityhopper from Rotterdam to London and rode to Brookplace, the beautiful estate in Chobham that is currently a Christian center for spiritual formation and communication. I was given a small cottage, all for myself!

Now I am ready to write about the complex history of Ukraine. After all I have read, one thing is clear: without a good knowledge of history the present situation of that country will only puzzle and confuse a visitor.

I need to have at least a basic outline of the millennium of Christianity in Ukraine in my head in order to "place" all that I will see and hear in the weeks to come. Let me try to summarize the core moments of the last thousand years!

In AD 988 Christianity came from Constantinople to Kyivan Rus', a medieval state centered at Kyiv and encompassing what is today Ukraine, Belarus, and European Russia. With the baptism of Prince Vladimir and his people, Rus' accepted the Byzantine liturgical and spiritual tradition. Although the developing rift between the East and West did not involve Kyiv directly, the Rus' Church ended up on the side of Constantinople. This schism was finalized by the Crusaders' sack of Constantinople in 1204. Thus the country now known as Ukraine became a part of the Orthodox half of Christendom.

Since then many attempts were made to reestablish unity between Rome and Constantinople, but little has been resolved. On the contrary, tensions and conflicts have only grown.

In 1596 at the Synod of Brest-Litovsk, most of the Church leadership in Ukraine and Belarus, then living under the political influence of Poland and Lithuania, recognized the pope as head of the Church, while keeping their Eastern-Rite liturgy. Today, the heirs of the Union of Brest live mostly in western Ukraine. Over the centuries the Synod of Brest led to enormous conflicts between Orthodox Christians and so-called Uniates, not just with those who adopted the Eastern Rite, but also between Eastern (Greek) and Western (Latin) Catholics. In 1946, at a mock synod choreographed by the Stalin regime, the Eastern Rite Catholic Church (the Greek Catholic Church) was suppressed and its believers forced to become part of the Orthodox Church under the leadership of the Patriarch of Moscow. This forced the Greek Catholic Church underground.

Since the perestroika of Gorbachev, and especially since the dissolution of the Soviet Union and the independence of Ukraine, the Greek Catholic Church has reemerged in great vitality with a complete hierarchy, priests, religious communities, and laity. The Greek Catholic Church not only survived the persecution but was, in some ways, even strengthened by it.

But this reemergence of the Greek Catholic Church has led to new conflicts with the Orthodox Church as well as some tensions with the Roman authorities. The Orthodox Church was hostile to the reclaiming of former church property, and the Church of Rome was perceived as having insufficient respect for the long-suffering of the underground Church and its desire to develop into maturity within the Catholic communion, fostering Eastern theological, ecclesiological, and disciplinary traditions. Meanwhile the Orthodox Church itself became increasingly divided. There is the independent

Ukrainian Autocephalous Orthodox Church, the Ukrainian Orthodox Church under the Patriarch of Moscow, and more recently the new "Ukrainian Orthodox Church–Kyivan Patriarchate." The latter consists of former members of the Autocephalous Ukrainian Orthodox Church (AUOC) and the Ukrainian Orthodox Church (UOC). At present there is no sign of reconciliation among the three jurisdictions.

All of this means that today there are at least five church bodies: the Greek Catholic Church, the Latin Catholic Church, the Autocephalous Orthodox Church, the Orthodox Church under the Moscow Patriarchate, and the Orthodox Church–Kyivan Patriarchate. [Henri does not mention the numerous Protestant and non-Christian religious communities.] These many divisions reflect the long history of conflicts between Ukraine and Poland, Ukraine and Russia, and Ukraine and Rome. Since the political independence of Ukraine, these conflicts, always simmering beneath the surface of the country's religious life, have reemerged with renewed bitterness, and even violence.

Both Zenia and Borys are active members of the Greek Catholic Church. Their families left Ukraine during the Stalinist takeover of western Ukraine, and they have lived their religious lives in Eastern Rite parishes in North America. Nathan and I are both members of the Western Catholic Church. I was born in it; Nathan was received into it as an adult. Happily, we have a great respect and love for each other's traditions, spirituality, and liturgy. As is often the case, understanding, respect, and support seem easier to come to "in exile" than at home where the conflicts found their origins.

Chobham—Tuesday, July 27, 1993

Reflecting on the history of Ukraine, I am overwhelmed by the long-suffering of its people. It seems that there never has been a time without oppression and exploitation. For an outsider, it looks as if the Ukrainian people have always been used by some outside power, whether Mongol, Russian, Polish, Lithuanian, Austrian, or German [Romanian and Hungarian].

The twentieth century is likely the most oppressive of all centuries in Ukrainian history. I have always known about the Holocaust as the blackest hour of our age. But now, after listening to Borys and reading different articles and books, I know that during World War I and the subsequent failed struggle for Ukrainian independence (1914–1920), between 2 and 3 million people died. Now I also know that during the year 1932–33 close to 4 million Ukrainians were starved to death when Stalin withheld food from the people to force them into submission, and that during World War II, when Nazi and Russian troops moved through Ukraine in rapid succession, close to 7 million inhabitants of Ukraine lost their lives. Now I know that in the 1930s virtually the entire political and cultural elite of eastern Ukraine was summarily executed or deported to death camps, and that during the 1950s hundreds of thousands of inhabitants of western Ukraine were forcibly sent to Siberia. Now I know that in the thirty years between 1929 and 1959, some 15 million Ukrainians perished due to war, famine, and political, cultural, and religious purges. The most recent disaster visited upon Ukraine was the Chernobyl nuclear accident, which has contaminated a large region of northern Ukraine and Belarus. And now I know that until very recently most Ukrainians have never enjoyed real freedom. The immense suffering of the Ukrainian people is not as well known to the Western world as the immense suffering of the Jewish people, but it is no less real.

Against this background I can better understand the centrality of long-suffering in the spirituality of the Ukrainian people. Happiness, prosperity, physical well-being, success, and esteem have not been part of the experience of most Ukrainians, especially the peasants. For them these "gifts of freedom" have always belonged to the future kingdom, of which they were able to catch only a glimpse in their splendid liturgies. The Ukrainian people have always been waiting people, waiting not just for the oppressors to leave their country, but also waiting for the fulfillment of the divine promise of eternal joy and peace.

Chobham—Wednesday, July 28, 1993

I have been thinking a great deal about the deep influence of Eastern Christian spirituality on my own life. It started to dawn on me that my love of prayer, the liturgical life, and sacred art, especially icons, were all greatly nurtured by the Christian East. I had almost forgotten this; here I am, full of ambivalence, and even fear, before a trip to Ukraine, while in fact I am going to the country from which some of the greatest spiritual gifts have come to me! Maybe I have allowed the many ecclesiastical conflicts I have been reading about to hide, temporarily, the great beauty this country holds for me. Instead of being apprehensive and a little anxious about this journey, I should be deeply grateful for being able, finally, to go to the source of much of my own spiritual life. It should be a pilgrimage!

Thinking of my trip as a pilgrimage, I recall the famous book about the Jesus Prayer, *The Way of the Pilgrim*, that has had such a deep effect on me. It is the story of a simple peasant who walked through the country visiting holy places in Ukraine, all the while reciting the Jesus Prayer: "Lord Jesus Christ, have mercy on me." This prayer gradually "moved" from his lips to his heart until it had become one with his breathing. Finally he could say: "I am not praying the prayer, but the prayer prays in me." Wherever this peasant went, he radiated love, kindness, and goodness and—to his own delight—saw how people's lives changed through meeting him. It is a charming, often humorous eighteenth-century story that gives expression, in a narrative way, to the rich tradition of the prayer of the heart, also called the *hesychastic* tradition (from the Greek *hesychazein,* to rest).

The hesychastic tradition finds its origin in the Egyptian desert during the fourth and fifth centuries. There the desert fathers and desert mothers, living in the spirit of St. Anthony, recited the Jesus Prayer to bring them to a complete, holy rest with God in the heart. In the sixth century we find this spiritual tradition in full bloom in the monasteries on Mount Sinai, and in the tenth century on Mount Athos in Greece. From Mount Athos it finds its way to what, today, is Ukraine and Russia and blossomed not only in monasteries but also among the Orthodox laity.

The main writings of this hesychastic tradition are compiled in the *Philokalia*. During the eighteenth and nineteenth centuries the prayer of the heart (the Jesus Prayer) was the favorite prayer not only among the monks of the Christian East but also among individuals, like the peasant who told his story in *The Way of the Pilgrim*. The monk Chariton put together a book of excerpts of these mystical writings that was later translated into English and published under the title *The Art of Prayer*. Few books on prayer have had such a lasting influence on me as this book. Thomas Merton, the Trappist monk and well-known American spiritual writer, considered *The Art of Prayer* the most significant book on prayer he knew. I fully agree with him.

My own prayer life has many ups and downs, but somehow the prayer "Lord Jesus Christ, have mercy on me" is always there—even during my driest periods. In its utter simplicity and profound compactness, it keeps me connected with Jesus, especially during times when little else will.

My great love for the liturgical life also has much to do with Eastern Christianity. Although I live and worship in the West and am daily nurtured by the Latin-Rite Eucharist, my occasional contact with the Liturgy of St. John Chrysostom has given me a deep understanding of living in the world without being of it. Indeed, participating in these liturgies has given me a sense of being in heaven before leaving earth. There too did I discover icons, not as illustrations, decorations, or ornaments, but as true windows on the eternal. At first these sacred images seemed distant and somewhat forbidding, but as I started to pray before them, they gradually revealed their secrets to me and led me far beyond my daily preoccupations into the kingdom of God.

I have received so much from my Christian brothers and sisters in the Eastern Churches. And it's possible that only a few of them are aware of their own richness because of the horrendous suppression and persecution they have endured during the past century. But now, when new freedom finally emerges, this sacred heritage can be reclaimed and become an even richer source of renewal for the whole Christian world.

Chobham—Thursday, July 29, 1993

Everything went according to schedule. Nathan and Borys both arrived on time. Tonight we called Zenia in Lviv, and her excitement seems even greater than ours.

I keep having a deep feeling that this journey is full of promise, that something very important is in store for us, something that will gradually become clear. When Nathan embraced me at the airport, a new joy filled my whole being, and when Borys with a big grin on his face walked into Brookplace an hour later, I thought, *It is all happening. It is not just a dream. It's all real, not just an illusion.* I am used to expecting more than what is possible, but today it feels as if more is possible than I expect.

Chobham—Friday, July 30, 1993

Last evening Borys gave us a "lecture" on the history of Ukraine. With the help of *Ukraine: A Historical Atlas*, he showed us the gradual emergence of the Ukrainian nation as it appears today. Three years jumped out from his presentation, three years that I want to remember: 1204, 1453, and 1589. All three years are connected with Constantinople. In 1204 the Crusaders (Franks from the West) sacked this beautiful city, rich in culture and spiritual life. This brutal act created the still-lasting division between the Christian West and the Christian East. Not even the mutual excommunications by Pope Leo IX and Patriarch Michael Caerularius in 1054 had represented such a decisive moment in the schism between East and West. Until the sacking of Constantinople by the Crusaders, the way to reconciliation was still open, but the ruthless destruction of 1204 changed all that. Even today Greco-Orthodox people refer, in angry moments, to Western Christians as "Franks."

In 1453 Constantinople fell again, this time to the Turks. They were able to break through the enormous wall that protected the city from invaders and subject it to Muslim rule. A few years earlier, at the Council of Florence in 1439, a serious attempt had been made to restore the unity between Constantinople and Rome. Although part of Constantinople's desire for unity was connected with the hope for military support in this conflict with the Turks, there was also a serious theological and spiritual motivation at work. Ultimately the council's efforts ended in failure, and the gulf between the Eastern and Western Churches continued and deepened.

The year 1589 is the third important date. In that year, the Patriarch of Constantinople was forced to elevate Moscow to a patriarchate. This was the result of the state of disarray in which the Patriarchate of Constantinople found itself and the increasing poverty of the Greek Church under Ottoman rule. At first, Greek priests and bishops went north to Ukrainian and Belarusian lands and Muscovy to beg for financial support. Then, finally, the Patriarch himself went on a fundraising mission. When he came to Moscow the Muscovites put him under house arrest and would not release him until he had first raised the Metropolitan of Moscow to the status of Patriarch. He gave in to their demand, received enough money to build a new church or two, and returned to Constantinople. In 1686 the Orthodox Metropolitan of Kyiv was placed under the direction of the Patriarch of Moscow. Thus Kyiv lost its ecclesiastical subordination with Constantinople.

These three events, all reflecting the decline of Constantinople, deeply affected the spiritual and ecclesiastical life of present-day Ukraine. In 988, when the emissaries of Prince Vladimir went to Constantinople, the splendor of the Byzantine liturgies so attracted them that they brought that form of Christianity back with them. Six centuries later, all of the Byzantine splendor had gone. Constantinople had become Istanbul, a Muslim city with a poor Christian minority. Meanwhile Moscow had become the center of power in the Eastern Christian world. This shift had far-reaching consequences for the way the Orthodox Church in Ukraine developed during the following centuries.

Chobham—Saturday, July 31, 1993

Late last night Borys returned from a short trip to London where he had given a lecture to the Ukrainian Greek Catholic community. He was seeking interest and support for the Theological Academy of Lviv, which was closed by the Soviets in 1944 and will be reopened in 1994. Borys is the chairman of the preparatory committee of this renewed ecumenically oriented institute of learning. It was clear to me that Borys was somewhat disappointed by the reception he found. Only twenty-five people came; they showed less interest in church affairs than in the political and economic crisis in Ukraine and were generally wary of new projects.

Since the independence of Ukraine and the new openness to the West, thousands of Ukrainians have traveled abroad seeking support from their Ukrainian brothers and sisters. At first they were received with open arms, but now they are sometimes treated as burdensome fundraisers.

I better be prepared to be looked upon in Lviv as a wealthy Westerner who has more than I deserve. I know that I easily get impatient when people relate to me primarily as someone who can help them out. I know this from my experiences in Bolivia and Peru, where people often showed more interest in my financial support than in my spiritual message.

Still, all of this brings me face-to-face with the enormous injustice in our world. It is important that I go beyond my little irritations and feelings of being used and manipulated and realize the truth that there will never be peace without justice. From the point of view of the poor, I am unjustly rich!

Lviv—Sunday, August 1, 1993

What a day! At 8 a.m., Eucharist at Bart and Patricia's home. At 8:45 a.m., a taxi to Heathrow Airport. At 10:50 a.m., with LOT Airlines to Warsaw and from Warsaw to Lviv. At 5:20 p.m. (local time), welcomed by Zenia and friends at Lviv Airport. At 7 p.m. we were at the Dnister Hotel. At 7:30 p.m., celebration of welcome by the Faith and Light communities of Lviv. At 9:45 p.m., dinner at Dnister Hotel. At 11 p.m., to bed.

When I write it down this way, it seems as if there was nothing very special about the day. Everything went according to schedule! But beneath this schedule was the huge move from the West to the East; from great wealth to great poverty; from crowded roads to empty streets; from busy, self-confident people to tired and depressed-looking men and women; from a liturgy around the dining room table to the melancholy Vespers in a makeshift chapel amid a large, gray housing development. It is hard to express in words this move from one world to another.

The very first impressions are: dark, empty, depressed, shy, slow, poor, fearful, and somber. When the plane landed at the Lviv airport, we noticed the old broken-down planes on the side of the runway, the boarded-up houses in the distance, and the old-looking oil trucks at the terminal. The terminal itself was like a decrepit, unkempt bus station. All the passengers were crowded into a little waiting room, wondering how long it would take to get through the passport control and customs. Borys made us feel safe; without his presence, Nathan and I would have felt lost. Although we were the first to leave the plane it took an hour to fill out papers, have our documents stamped, and find our luggage. As we waited, we looked at the huge painting on the wall, showing us proud Communist men and women marching with large red flags. Nathan asked Borys, "Why do they still have that painting there?" Borys replied, "They just don't have the money to commission a new one!"

When we finally made it to the arrival hall, Zenia welcomed us warmly with beautiful dahlias. Then we all drove to the city. The first thing we noticed was how little traffic there was on the streets—few cars and few people. I felt like shouting, "Where is everybody? This is supposed to be a big city!" After driving through the suburbs, with their large, miserable-looking high-rises and many half-finished buildings and bridges, we entered the old city of Lviv, founded in the mid-thirteenth century. The center showed its old glory: Viennese-style buildings along romantic-looking, cobbled streets. This was the city fashioned when it was part of the Austro-Hungarian Empire: eighteenth- and nineteenth-century Austrian architecture, reminiscent of the elegant style of the Hapsburgs. But the atmosphere is no longer festive. At 7 p.m. there is scarcely anyone on the street.

Here and there a little group of people stand in line at a bus station. "Where is the shopping center?" I asked Zenia. She laughed. "There is no shopping center. There are only a few food shops here and there; people don't have the money to buy more than the bare necessities."

Our hotel is big and somber. It is a typical product of the Soviet era: heavy, square, formal, and foreboding. As we entered, there was barely any light. "Electricity is scarce in the city," Zenia said. "But you will, at least, have running water here! That's a luxury!" I looked around and was struck by the solemnity of the place: dark wood paneling and much marble. The hotel is a leftover of heavy-handed Soviet domination. "Many of the Soviet monuments are gone," Zenia explained, "but hotels like this remind you that it has been only a few years since Ukraine became free."

We unpacked and freshened up. "Let's go," Zenia said. "Our Faith and Light communities are waiting to welcome you to Ukraine; they have prepared a surprise for you!" I was very tired and not really in the mood for anything new—bad or good. I just wanted to go to bed. But it was clear that Zenia had something waiting for us that we couldn't ignore.

Vladzio drove us back to the suburbs. There, in the midst of the large, gray apartment buildings was a little chapel. Zenia commented, "In the fall of 1990, the Greek Catholic people of the area decided to build their own church. First they set up a large plastic tent. Then, in the spring of 1991, they built their own little wooden chapel. Now they are building a large church."

As we drove to the chapel, we could see the unfinished walls of the new church. I said, "That's going to be a huge place." Borys replied, "Sure, if they ever finish it. A few years ago things were still cheap and easy to get, but now there is no money and no material to continue. Work on the church is almost at a standstill." [The church is finished and is most impressive.]

When we parked the van, we saw a few hundred people standing outside the chapel looking in. The first words I heard were, "Hospody pomyluy" (Lord have mercy, Lord have mercy). They are the only words I know of the Eastern-Rite liturgy. I have known them since I was seventeen years old, and now I hear them again. It's the "Kyrie Eleison," the heart of the Jesus Prayer, the most frequently used words in the liturgy of the Eastern Church. I was moved to hear them. It seemed that they introduced me to this new country in the best way. "Lord have mercy": the prayer of God's people, the prayer that has sounded through the centuries of struggle, wars, persecution, and oppression. They are words of the liturgy. But they are also words belonging to the most intimate prayer of the heart. I say them often, even without much consciousness: when I cannot fall asleep, when I walk or drive my car, when I am waiting for someone. It's the simplest and most profound prayer. It's the prayer that binds all of Christianity together. It's the prayer that summarizes all prayer. "Lord Jesus"—Lord of all we are and have—"have mercy": show us your forgiveness, your kindness, your healing grace.

We waited until the liturgy had finished. As people were leaving, Nathan and I walked into the little church. Many women and a few men stood there singing the Vespers with the priests. With great strength and conviction they sang the beautiful, harmonious psalmodies. When we left, Nathan said, "People look so serious, tired, and discouraged. Their faces show a lot of pain and suffering. There is little joy." I felt what he said. These are people who have lived a life very different from our own. They have lived hunger, fear, poverty, and much long-suffering. They have been busy just surviving. Their "Lord have mercy" comes from hearts that have been tested for many decades.

With a "Let's go," Zenia interrupted our reflections and took us to a little field a few hundred feet from the church entrance. "Here are your friends waiting to welcome you." As we came close, I saw several wheelchairs and about a hundred people gathered around them. Two brightly colored signs were held up: one said, "Welcome Nathan," the other, "Welcome Henri."

Fr. Henri is greeted with bread and salt.

Nathan Ball (left) and Fr. Henri (right) receive flowers of welcome.
Zenia Kushpeta (center) interprets the exchange.

At once I sensed that this was a special group. There was excitement, expectation, and joy on their faces—and many smiles. They looked us right in the eyes without embarrassment or fear. They stood there in a half circle waiting for Zenia, Borys, Nathan, and I to come close. Then Zenia started to speak with her familiar upbeat voice. I didn't understand her Ukrainian but could easily pick up that she was talking about Nathan and me having come from Canada to visit Faith and Light in Lviv. People listened to her with great attentiveness and happy amazement. Then, when Zenia stopped speaking, a woman in a lovely Ukrainian dress came forward and handed us a large, richly decorated Ukrainian bread. Both Nathan and I were asked to break off a piece, dip it in salt, and eat it. It was the traditional Ukrainian gesture of welcome.

Then all the handicapped men and women came forward with their families and friends and offered us flowers, pictures, icons, and pins. Soon the two of us were standing there with large bouquets of roses, carnations, and other flowers, trying to hold on to them as one after the other person gave us more and more and more. There were handshakes, kisses, embraces, and many welcomes. We kept saying, "Thank you, thank you," and after a quick word with Borys, "Dya-ku-yu," the Ukrainian word for "Thank you."

There was Vasyl, a young handicapped man, who kept embracing me, saying, "Welcome, welcome." There was Yurchyk in his wheelchair, looking at us with a radiant smile. There were Vadik, Olezhyk, and Sofia, all full of excitement at being part of this celebration of welcome. I looked at Nathan and saw how deeply moved he was. His face was full of amazement, gratitude, and joy. I just marveled at it all. Here, amid these gray, somber buildings, was this little group of handicapped men and women with their families and friends creating a small island of pure joy and peace.

Zenia took up her guitar, and everyone joined her in singing, "Alleluia, alleluia." It was a little piece of heaven on earth! As I looked up to the high-rise buildings around us, I suddenly noticed hundreds of people looking at us from their balconies. They seemed to gaze at us with a mixture of curiosity, loneliness, and a desire to belong.

Father Stefan, a priest who had recently discovered Faith and Light through his daughter and was obviously deeply touched by this new sign of hope, spoke a few words, and Father Petro, who had led the liturgy in the chapel, also came forward and offered a brief homily. There were more songs, more gifts, and more speeches. There were drinks and all sorts of baked goods. People were happy, playful, and full of good spirits.

Finally, it was time to go. We all formed a large circle. The curious onlookers came closer and joined the circle that became wider and wider. I asked one of the older women who had stood silently behind me to enter the circle. She was glad to be invited, as were the others. As we held hands we prayed together the Our Father. After the Amen, people embraced each other with the words, "Peace be with you." I was amazed at how easily the "curious onlookers" became part of this exchange of peace. Many elderly women gave me kisses on both cheeks, and their serious, pain-filled faces broke open into large smiles.

"Let's go," Zenia said. "You guys need some rest." She was very right. I was exhausted but with a better exhaustion than that of a few hours earlier. By 9:45 p.m. we were back at the hotel. After a quiet dinner, while Borys left to go home, Nathan, Zenia, and I kept talking until 11 p.m. I could hardly believe that we had been in Ukraine for only a few hours.

Lviv—Monday, August 2, 1993

This afternoon, Borys took Nathan and me for a walk through the city park. I sensed a very different atmosphere from yesterday. After crossing the park, we walked into the beautiful center of the old city. The stately houses with their richly decorated façades, the large trees and the green boulevards, the cobblestone streets with their old-fashioned red and yellow streetcars, and the many people, young and old, going their different ways under a bright sun created a very homey feeling.

Fr. Henri gets to know the city of Lviv (Svoboda Avenue, downtown Lviv).

We walked past the university [Ivan Franko National University of Lviv], crossed the splendid Freedom Prospect Boulevard with the newly erected statue of Taras Shevchencko (the great nineteenth-century poet whose verse codified the modern Ukrainian language), visited the Roman Catholic cathedral, walked around the city hall with its four mythological statues, admired the beautiful tower of the Church of the Dormition [the Korniakt Tower], and climbed the little hill topped by St. Michael's Church and the Studite Monastery.

Lviv showed itself to us in all its gentle beauty. A gem of a city: colorful, full of history, and now with a new vitality. At many places, restorations were going on. Statues and fountains were being cleaned; cracked walls were being repaired; discolored façades were receiving a facelift; and all over, there was work going on to make the city look new and fresh again. Only two years had passed since independence, but with the aid of many different countries and cultural foundations, the city was already regaining some of its old glory. "Imagine!" Borys said, as we walked around city hall, "when you come back in a few years, this place will be full of tourists from all over the world and you will see it again in the festive splendor of a century ago."

At the Studite Monastery, Borys took us to his office where he does his research on the underground Church. He introduced us to Oksana and Donata, two of his coworkers, and explained his research project to us. Within the next five years he and sixteen assistants plan to conduct two thousand interviews to document the way the Greek Catholic Church survived underground from 1946 until 1990. Very little has been written down. Only by taking the oral history from the bishops, priests, religious, and laity can the story of the persecution under the Soviet regime be written.

As an example, Borys told us about Father Josafat Kavatsiv, a fearless, bold, and very courageous priest who traveled far and wide to keep in touch with Greek Catholic Christians, to conduct services in their homes and, sometimes, even in front of their closed churches. Father Josafat received his formation and was ordained in the underground Church. His daring behavior finally led to his arrest and imprisonment by the Soviet authorities in 1980. He remained a prisoner for five years.

Borys described him as a strong character with great integrity but pointed out that his uncompromising attitude toward the Soviet regime also made him quite hostile toward the Orthodox Church. He is very bitter about the priests who did join the Orthodox Church after the mock synod in 1946 and who, after independence, were welcomed back and given positions in the Greek Catholic community. After all he had experienced in the underground Church and in Soviet prisons, ecumenism is certainly not his ideal! [At the end of his life Fr. Kavatsiv claimed that he was a bishop—ordained by Bishop Oleksandr Khira in Kazakhstan in 1980. The UGCC commission was unable to find evidence of this fact. Thus, the acts of Fr. Kavatsiv as bishop were invalid, and he was excommunicated. Fr. Kavatsiv died in 2010.]

The story of Josafat Kavatsiv clearly reveals the complex situation of the postindependence Ukrainian Churches. There was horrendous suffering and painful betrayals, and there were moments of heroic faithfulness and moments of rigid refusals to cooperate. Most of all, there are long memories that make it hard to forget and forgive.

We concluded our tour with a short visit to the offices of Beacon Press. We were warmly received by the director, Bohdan Trojanowski, and two of his coworkers. He explained to us that the aim of Beacon is to publish and distribute books, periodicals, and other materials that will foster the development of Christian values among the people of Ukraine. Many of their publications are translations of pastoral, moral, and spiritual books from Germany, France, or the United States. During the Soviet era, hardly anything of a religious nature was written or published in Ukraine. I was happy to see two of my books, *Out of Solitude* and *Making All Things New*, among their publications. Borys assured me that the translation was excellent.

On the way home, we took a streetcar, where we observed an interesting "tradition." Money was passed on from person to person going from the back of the streetcar to the driver in the front, and tickets returning from the driver to the back. So money and tickets were constantly going from hand to hand in different directions. We wondered how people could dare to give their money to complete strangers and trust to get back the tickets they needed.

Later, in the hotel, Zenia said, "There are some very solid customs among the people. This is one of them; another is always to give your seat to the elderly and to children. Nobody would ever steal ticket money in a streetcar. It's a sacred ritual!"

Lviv—Tuesday, August 3, 1993

Every morning, Nathan, Borys, and I get together in Nathan's room and Borys gives us a little more history. I don't know how any of the things we see or hear would make sense without a basic knowledge of history. The roots of what grows above ground are long and deep, and knowing them helps us to become better observers without too many prejudices, quick judgments, easy solutions, or facile evaluations.

Today, Borys spoke about the twentieth-century history of the Greek Catholic Church. He focused on the two main personalities of the period: Andrei Sheptytsky and Josyf Slipyj. Andrei Sheptytsky was Metropolitan of Lviv from 1901 to 1944. His successor as head of the Greek Catholic Church in Ukraine [1944-1984], Josyf Slipyj, lived in Soviet prisons and Siberian exile from 1945 until 1963, and then in Rome until his death in 1984.

Sheptytsky—the tall, aristocratic mystic, spiritual writer, reformer, and founder of many cultural and intellectual institutions—and Slipyj—the bright, strong-willed scholar, confessor, and staunch defender of the Ukrainian cause—have inspired countless Greek Catholics with a vision of an autonomous Ukrainian Church in communion with the pope of Rome. Their great gifts of heart and mind and their radical commitment to their country and their church have made them Ukrainian heroes of this century. The canonization process of Sheptytsky and the popular veneration of

Slipyj, shown especially when Slipyj's remains were brought back to Lviv in 1992, demonstrate the great role these church leaders played in the national consciousness of the people of western Ukraine.

After Borys's talk, we all walked to St. George's Greek Catholic Cathedral and visited the crypt where Sheptytsky and Slipyj are buried. It was a moving experience to see the tombs of these two great spiritual and national leaders.

Across from the cathedral, in the residence of Cardinal Myroslav Lubachivsky, we saw different paintings of his two famous predecessors. Borys explained that to Ukrainians the *Ostpolitik* (the Vatican policy of accommodation with the Eastern communist governments) and the present-day centrist tendencies of Rome have not been encouraging for those who want to deepen and strengthen the vision of Sheptytsky and Slipyj. Slipyj began to use the title of Patriarch for himself in 1975, thus expressing the hope of the Greek Catholic Ukrainian community to be affirmed by the pope in its ecclesial identity in the face of the Soviet declaration that the church had ceased to exist. Slipyj became the standard-bearer for those Ukrainians who saw their church as a sister church in the universal communion of local churches, striving to be Orthodox *and* Catholic: an Eastern Church administered by a synod, headed by a patriarch, yet in full communion with Rome.

Walking into the cathedral and through the chancery office and the cardinal's residence put much flesh and bones on the stories we had just heard.

Visiting Saint George Cathedral and the residence of the Lviv metropolitans. Left to right: Borys Gudziak, Nathan Ball, Fr. Henri Nouwen, and Mykola Svarnyk.

In the afternoon we entered a very different world. Zenia's friend Mykola took us to his home. He lives on the sixth floor of one of the many high-rises at the outskirts of the city. He has a small apartment where he lives with his fourteen-year-old daughter, Mariana, and his severely handicapped five-year-old son, Andriiko. His wife died at Andriiko's birth. Here we got a glimpse of the daily life of most Ukrainian people. Very little space, few facilities for the little boy, and every little corner filled with books and papers. With some effort, all of us were able to fit around the table and enjoy each other's company. I was moved by the beautiful face of Andriiko and his generous smiles. Nathan asked Mykola about his work for the people with cerebral palsy and their families. Mykola showed his files with the names of all those with whom he was in contact, and told of his many efforts to find an office for the training facilities of his four-year-old organization, Nadiia (hope).

Visiting the apartment of Mykola Svarnyk. Fr. Henri
plays with Mykola's son Andriy.

Considering the many economic problems of the country, it is unlikely that handicapped people will easily make it to the priority list of the government agencies. Realistically speaking, financial as well as organizational support has to come from nongovernmental sources and mostly from other countries. A lot of goodwill and a lot of energy go into working for the poor and the handicapped, but also much frustration. Simple survival requires so much time and work that it is very hard to pay much attention to people with special needs.

Still, sitting in Mykola's apartment with little Andriiko cooing in my arms, I felt deeply grateful to be a part of the beginning of something very beautiful. I keep forgetting how Jean Vanier, the founder of L'Arche, started his first home for two mentally handicapped men in 1964 in France. It was so little and so primitive. But the vision and the love of those who started it allowed them to overcome many obstacles and to build up a network of communities that today are well established and a source of light and hope for many.

And now, here we are with Zenia, who during less than two years built up three Faith and Light groups in Lviv and is starting a fourth one in the city of Ternopil; and here we are with Mykola, who started Nadiia four years ago and has built up a network of close to one thousand families who have children with cerebral palsy. Their enormous dedication and deep faith are certainly able to do what Jean Vanier did. Both Nathan and I felt very inspired by what we heard and saw, and we both experienced a real desire to support and help Zenia and Mykola as much as we could.

At the end of the afternoon, we visited an orphanage for small children. Zenia brought us to the room with handicapped children. It is hard to describe what we saw. The little boy I took out of the large playpen where he was sitting with five other little children, without any toys, clung to me with such intensity that I didn't even know how to put him back. I felt very guilty just to offer him a little affection and then leave him again.

In the little beds, beautiful, small faces looked at us with such a desire for attention, love, and care that I felt like taking them all with me and starting a new L'Arche home on the spot.

Natalie, one of the little girls, evoked deep emotions in Zenia, who had visited her often in the past. Zenia had hoped to offer her a home but had been unable to. The little girl looked at her with eyes of despair, as if saying, "Is anyone going to take me out of here and give me a home? Is anyone going to love me enough to do more than just visit me and then leave me here?"

Lviv—Wednesday, August 4, 1993

A visit to the little fruit and vegetable market in downtown Lviv gave Nathan and me an idea of the poverty of the people. At the entrance to the marketplace, men and women were holding whatever they had to sell: a few potatoes, one or two cabbages, or some old kitchenware. Quite a few women were selling flowers and plastic shopping bags. As we entered the enclosed area with different stalls, more food was available: plums, blueberries, and peaches, but all of it in small amounts. It seems that little was being sold. "For most people it is too expensive," Borys said. "They can't afford to come here and buy fruits and vegetables. Most people only earn between thirty or forty thousand coupons [the transitional 'currency'] a month, which is between ten and fifteen dollars, and a pound of peaches cost a thousand coupons!" We also saw a few meat stalls. Borys continued, "Ten pounds of good meat would be a whole month's salary. You can understand that few people can come here."

To get some idea of the economic situation I have to realize that one day of work in Canada gives the same buying power as thirty days in Ukraine.

As we walked through the stalls, Nathan and I were struck by the tired-looking faces. Few smiles, few animated discussions. The general atmosphere was somber and heavy. Zenia said, "People look a lot older than they are. They work always. Many have come from their farms where they milk their cows and tend their little plots of land. They come far distances to sell their meager products. They grow old and tired very fast."

As we talked, we became aware of how victimized most Ukrainian peasants feel. They were always oppressed and exploited by one invader or another. It seemed that many of the peasants we saw at the marketplace lived with little hope for a better future. Independence had not brought them much progress. They were still very poor, hardly able to survive.

Fr. Henri, Nathan, and Borys visit a produce market in Lviv.

I have seen poverty in many places, especially in Central and Latin America, but the poverty in Ukraine strikes me as a poverty that has extinguished the spirit of the poor. The grateful and joyful smiles that gave me so much life in Latin America are absent here. Somewhere the spirit has been broken. We keep wondering whether the future will be any different. With so many voices in Russia wanting to reclaim Ukraine as part of their territory, there is the constant fear that independence might be a very fragile thing. The fact that the United States pays so much attention to Russia and so little to Ukraine, except in trying to have it give up its nuclear arsenal, makes Ukrainians question how much international support their independence will get when push comes to shove. The somber faces of the peasants certainly are not full of expectation for a better future.

After leaving the marketplace we hired a cab for two hours to visit two Faith and Light families. We first went to the Burdash family. Although we had not announced our coming, we found five family members at home: Ivanka and Bohdan, the parents; their children, Oleh and Ihor; and Ivanka's brother Myron. Ivanka's mother, who lives there, was not home. There are two rooms, one for the mother and Myron, and one for the parents and their two children. The little boy, Oleh, and his uncle Myron are both handicapped. The mother and her daughter Ivanka work in factories with a schedule that allows one of them to be home while the other works. Bohdan, the father, works in a television assembly factory, but now he was on vacation.

We were welcomed with open arms. It was clear how happy they were with our visit. We were led to the newly painted living room. Everything looked well cared for and very clean. On the walls were three large religious pictures, one of the Sacred Heart of Jesus, the other of the Sacred Heart of Mary, and the third one of the Guardian Angel protecting little children.

Nathan asked Ivanka to tell us about Faith and Light. She said, "With Oleh and Myron we felt very isolated. We couldn't go to church and had very few friends. But Zenia changed our life. She brought us in touch with other families with handicapped children and she even organized a Sunday each month when we all go together to church and have a meeting afterward. Now we are no longer isolated. Now we have friends, and now we go to different meetings and celebrations. Our lives certainly have changed." As she spoke, she looked gratefully at Zenia.

Oleh cannot speak, and Myron can only say a few words. For them there are no schools, day programs, or workplaces. They are always home and need to be cared for by the women in the family. Myron spends most of his time playing with the neighborhood children. Because of his handicap he is often laughed at and made fun of. But he is such a gentle man, radiating goodness and kindness. When I gave him a box of chocolates, he immediately shared them with all the people in the house. Later when we were visiting another family in the area, he came there to bring us beautiful roses from the little garden behind their house. Myron reminded me of the fools for Christ who are mentioned in many of the writings about the spiritual life of Eastern Christianity.

*Visiting "Faith and Light" families. Handicapped poet Andriy Shulha with
his mother, Fr. Henri, Nathan, Zenia Kushpeta, and Myron Pelekh.*

After our visit to the Burdash family we went to see Andriy,
a twenty-five-year-old man who was partially paralyzed as the
result of faulty injections received when he was three years old.
He is confined to a wheelchair and lives with his mother in a
small basement room. His father and his sister, with her family,
live in the upstairs part of the little house. In order to reach the
house, we had to go down quite a few steps from the main road.
There, Andriy was sitting on a little terrace outside his living
room. His mother was there with him. Nobody else was home.

Andriy was very excited to see us. His face was beaming.
He graciously accepted the fruit and flowers we had brought
for him and his mother. Soon he was telling his story: "For
most of my life I have been confined to my room. I saw the

outside world through my window. That's all I could see. Nobody could take me out of here, up the steps to the road, and into the city. It is too difficult, too tiring, and too complicated. I had no friends who came to visit. I was very alone. My mother had to do everything for me. But Zenia made a person of me. She gave me friends; she helped me get out of this place and meet other people. My life is so different now, thanks to God and thanks to Zenia."

Zenia, who did the translation, deliberately "undertranslated" the praise Andriy gave her, but Borys made sure that we knew that he literally said, "She made a person of me."

As we talked more with Andriy we became aware that he is a poet. We urged him to show us some of his work. His mother went into the room and returned with a notebook full of poems. Because of his speech impediment, Andriy couldn't read his own work, but Zenia read aloud a poem titled "The Wheelchair." Borys translated the whole poem into English, a poem about suffering and hope, confinement and deep longing, limitations and possibilities. The final verse was, "Will anyone ever ask me, 'Father, how are you doing?'" It still resounds in me as a succinct expression of Andriy's pain and his deep desire to live a fruitful life.

I asked, "Who wrote these poems in this notebook for you?" Andriy answered, "My thirteen-year-old nephew, Roman, takes dictation from me. He is able to understand me and write my poems for me. He is on vacation now, and my head is bursting with poems that I would like to dictate, but nobody else can do it as well as Roman." Andriy then lifted up the hand he still could use and showed us how he would be able to type his own poems if he had a typewriter. When we came home, we celebrated the Eucharist in Nathan's hotel room, and we shared with one another how we had experienced interiorly the events of which we had been a part.

☩

Lviv—Thursday, August 5, 1993

Zenia, Nathan, and I spent the afternoon visiting two families with handicapped children. We first went to the home of twelve-year-old Vadik and his mother, Maria. They live in an old apartment in the center of Lviv. Maria told us how she had simply occupied the place with her handicapped son after hearing that the previous occupant had died. This resulted in long legal battles with other people who claimed the same place—and much emotional turmoil. But the final outcome was victory for Vadik and Maria.

As we entered the large living room with its high ceiling, Vadik, lying on the carpet in the corner, greeted us with a beautiful smile. He was very excited to have visitors. Although his cerebral palsy severely handicapped him, he seemed very alert, intelligent, and good-natured. He followed our conversation with great attention and interest and was able to utter many words. As I looked at him and saw him struggle to express himself, I felt as though I were face-to-face with a young artist full of beautiful thoughts and ideas, but imprisoned in a body that did not allow him to let others know what was going on in his heart and mind.

Maria told us that her mother, who had spent much time with her grandson, had died a year ago. Maria had to give up her job and dedicate herself completely to Vadik's care. Concretely this meant that their only regular income came from Vadik's disability pension, which consisted of thirteen thousand coupons (three dollars) per month. Maria spends much of her time going from agency to agency begging for extra help. I have no idea how they survive, but somehow they seem to manage.

Vadik's greatest desire is to go to churches. There he feels happy, meets people, and prays. He urges his mother to take him to prayer services and liturgies.

Maria is a strong but also very demanding woman, and Vadik is all she has. There is no family to support her, and she is determined to get the best for her son. She wants young people to visit her son regularly, play with him, read to him, and help him with his mathematics. She wants money, attention, and time for Vadik, and she is willing to fight for it. Whenever she can she puts Vadik in his wheelchair, takes him down the long stone steps leading to the street level, and rides with him on the streetcars.

Speaking of God, Maria said, "Vadik has brought me back to God. He opened me to prayer, to the Bible, and to a belief in Jesus." As I held Vadik in my lap and lifted his head so that he could look straight at us, I sensed that this young handicapped boy was a true saint, a man of peace and love who had a very unique vocation in life. "He is a child of God," Maria said. "He has much to teach us."

I wish we could have stayed many hours with Vadik. Just being with him, holding him, listening to his few words, and telling him stories seemed such a privilege. But another family was waiting for us, and it was time to go.

We drove to the outskirts of Lviv and found the apartment where Mykhailyna lives with her husband and two handicapped boys, Andriy and Taras. Mykhailyna welcomed us warmly and led us to the living room where little eight-year-old Taras was lying on the sofa. I looked at his beautiful face and his small paralyzed body. His movements were very spastic, and his ability to make direct contact quite minimal. A little later Mykhailyna brought her other son, fourteen-year-old Andriy, to the living room. Like his younger brother, he is autistic, though he seemed less restless and anxious. Mykhailyna's husband wasn't home, but her two sisters and niece who lived in two neighboring apartments came over and joined us. They offered us some cognac, coffee, and delicious sandwiches. As the nine of us sat around the table, the three sisters told us their story.

In 1950 when they were still little children, their parents were evicted from their home and sent to Siberia. It was the time of Stalin's many purges. The argument used was that these people were being punished for their support of the Bandera independence movement, but in truth Stalin simply wanted to populate and exploit the mineral-rich areas of Siberia. To accomplish this he ordered 15 percent of the population from different regions of Ukraine, Lithuania, and other Soviet-dominated countries to be evacuated. Mykhailyna's family was dropped—together with thousands of other people from very diverse regions—in a Siberian forest and forced to make a life there. Many died, but Mykhailyna's family survived, and in 1956, after Stalin's death, they were allowed to return to Ukraine. There they built their own home, with a little garden. When, many years later, the high-rises were constructed around Lviv, they were forced to give up their home and accept the apartments the government had made available to them.

It was a story of persecution, manipulation, and victimization. Still, the three sisters were very strong and vital women, competing with each other to tell the best tale. Their main complaint now is the water. With two incontinent boys, needing constant changes of diapers, water is of the utmost importance. But the water is very polluted and hardly useable for cleaning. During certain times, there is no water at all.

As we asked more questions, it became clear that the boys never left the apartment. Mykhailyna said, "When we still had our own home with a garden, the boys could lie outside in the sun, but since we live in this eighth-floor apartment we can no longer take them out." I was surprised to hear that the main reason for not taking them out was not the difficulty in carrying them down, but their feelings of shame. Mykhailyna explained, "When they were still babies, we could take them out because nobody would notice the boys' handicaps, but now everyone will look at us and point at us. We don't want to be laughed at and to feel ashamed, so we keep them in the house."

The pale faces of Taras and Andriy proved that they had not seen the sun for a long time. I was struck by the great isolation that people with handicapped family members experience, and more than ever was convinced of the importance of Faith and Light.

Since we were having a special meeting for the parents of Faith and Light that same evening, we invited Mykhailyna to come. She promised to be there.

When we left, I knew that Taras and Andriy would remain part of my thinking and my concerns, and I wondered how we could play a little role in freeing them from their terrible isolation.

At 6 p.m. the parents of Faith and Light were invited for a meeting in one of the large rooms in the old Potocki Palace in downtown Lviv. It is a huge, stately building that evokes a bygone time of nobility, elegance, and great wealth. Today it is called the "Palace of Solemn Events." It is an empty building, with a few left-over pieces of furniture and an occasional rug on the floor—used mostly for civil ceremonies and registrations.

Twenty-four people came to the meeting—three men and twenty-one women. Zenia had invited them to meet Nathan and me and to listen to our stories. Borys was the translator. Nathan spoke about L'Arche and Daybreak, and I spoke about the gift of the handicapped people. We sang, prayed, and shared our ideas and feelings in small groups. It was a lively gathering, and it was a special joy to meet, once again, people whom we had visited in their homes: Ivanka, the mother of Oleh; the mother of the poet Andriy; Maria, the mother of Vadik; and Mykhailyna, the mother of Taras and Andriy.

Lviv—Friday, August 6, 1993

At noon, Nathan and I gave a little press conference for three Lviv journalists and a few friends of the Ukrainian Greek Catholic Youth for Christ organization and the Obnova (renewal) student movement. It was held in one of the small meeting rooms in the Palace of Solemn Events where we met last night. Nathan and I spoke for a few minutes about our reason for being in Ukraine, and the journalists asked about our financial situation in Canada, our plans for an ongoing relationship with Ukraine, our perspectives on handicapped people, and our attitude regarding the opinion that Jesus is the only way to salvation. It was a rather low-key event, but it will certainly bring some welcome publicity to Faith and Light in Lviv.

At 4 p.m. Vladzio, the driver, took Nathan, Zenia, Borys, and me to the summer camp at Novyi Rozdil, a good hour's drive south of Lviv. There Zenia had planned a weekend retreat for about a hundred people, mostly youth. During the trip, Vladzio explained to us a lot about "economics" in Ukraine. If people had to live on what they earn (for most people no more than ten dollars per month), nobody would survive. Even though a streetcar ticket costs less than one cent, and even though food prices are completely different from Western countries, an official salary simply isn't enough to live on. Still, wherever we went, people were managing and able to eat, clothe themselves, and often to have nice furniture, a television, and a few luxury items. Underneath the official salaries and prices, another economy makes this possible. It is an economy of bribes, favoritism, "procuring," and, most of all, connections with family and friends in the West. Nearly everyone seems to know someone who knows someone who somehow gets something from somewhere in the West. Coupons are worthless; what counts are dollars.

Vladzio told us proudly about his sixteen-year-old-daughter, an excellent student with very good marks. She very much wants to go to a business school in Lviv, but the only way to get in is with a bribe of seven hundred dollars. That is a fortune far beyond his means. It would take him more than twenty years to save such an amount. His only way is friends who have friends in the West.

"Well," we asked, "is your daughter going to make it?" With a grin Vladzio answered, "Sure, I borrowed the money."

While talking about the Ukrainian economies, we drove through an area with huge cement and sulfur factories. The air looked terribly polluted, and we wondered about the health of the children who grew up there. It turned out that the summer camp we were going to was built for these children.

Novyi Rozdil—Saturday, August 7, 1993

Seldom have I been with people who are so eager to learn about the spiritual life. For many years these men and women did not have an opportunity to meet freely for prayer, to speak openly about their faith, or to receive any form of religious instruction. Now it was possible, and they wanted it. Several hundred young people wanted to come, but many had to be disappointed. There were places for only one hundred. So strong was their desire to be part of this retreat that they were willing to make many sacrifices—both in money and time—to be there.

Being together, praying together, singing together, listening to words about the gospel, having good meals, a decent bed to sleep in and just feeling safe with one another—it was a heavenly experience for them. After half a day, many said, "I don't want to go home tomorrow! This is too good; please ask the buses not to pick us up so soon again! This is what we need, this is what we want!"

I was struck by the great vitality of the people. Most of them are in their twenties or thirties. They are intelligent, articulate, very cooperative, and deeply religious. They show their piety with great ease. They pray before and after meals with sincere devotion, they come together to say the rosary, they love holy cards, and they sing the beautiful melodies of the liturgy with great conviction.

*Fr. Henri, Nathan Ball, and Zenia Kushpeta with the employees of the Church
History Institute headed by Borys Gudziak: Natalia Klymovska, Donata
Bobryk, and Iryna Kolomyets, and Borys's cousin Teodor's wife Oksana and
daughter Orysia during the retreats in Novyi Rozdil (August 1993).*

It was a wonderful group of people: university students, publishers, researchers, actors from a theatre company, youth workers, radio programmers, seminarians, women religious, and young mothers of busy families. There was no sign of cynicism or skepticism. Nobody questioned the value of the retreat, the importance of the gospel, and the significance of the church.

In many ways I felt as if I were back in Holland in the 1950s when being devout and churchgoing was not only acceptable but supported and admired by family and friends. In the Catholic circles where I grew up, daily rosary, the Stations of the Cross, a deep devotion to Mary, a great love for the saints, and a strong desire to listen to teachers and preachers who would inspire our faith—all of that was a normal, integrated part of my daily life.

Nevertheless, it is clear that these retreatants form a very select group. Millions of people in Ukraine are not going to any church. There is a lot of indifference, depression, and despair. Alcoholism is rampant, there are many abortions and divorces, and the general mood of the country is still pervaded with feelings of suspicion, resentment, and jealousy.

But the people who came to the retreat are the best people Ukraine has to build a new country and to live toward a better future—and after the long years of Soviet control, the church is the place for them to find inspiration and hope.

How long will this last? The West with all its wealth and opportunities is coming closer each day, and it is not clear whether these young, energetic, and spiritually alive people will be able to hold on to their faith, traditions, and spiritual ideals when they discover that being religious in the West doesn't have the same avant-garde quality as in Ukraine. But one thing is clear: this is the right time to offer formation, training, vision, and inspiration. Strangely enough, that has to come from the West—because what comes from the West is "in"! I was amazed at how much authority was given to Zenia, Borys, Nathan, and myself. We came from the West, and when we speak with conviction about spiritual matters we have a greater credibility than Ukrainian spiritual leaders.

What kind of formation is necessary? My personal feeling is that what Ukrainian leaders need is to discover the empowering quality of the Gospels. The values they know are humility, long-suffering patience, endurance, and obedience. The values they do not know are self-reliance, freedom, proclamation, and mission. When I had spoken for an hour about the importance of "claiming our Belovedness" and "proclaiming to others their Belovedness," a young Ukrainian came up to me with Thomas à Kempis's *Imitation of Christ* in his hand and showed me the text that says that we are "nothing" and can live a good spiritual life only when we never forget our nothingness. He was quite perplexed about my positive view of the human person. Staying within his own frame of reference, I explained to him that God had "looked down on the humiliation of his servants" and lifted us up to greatness by revealing to us that we are as beloved as his own son, Jesus. I tried to explain to him that we are called to live not from the place where we think about ourselves as nothing, useless, or sinful, but from the place of our rebirth, the place where we can claim our new identity as the chosen children of God. I think he understood my words but was far from truly accepting them.

There is little doubt in my mind that the Eastern spirituality, notwithstanding its glorious liturgies and its emphasis on the light of Mount Tabor (the light that comes to us through the prayer of the heart), is predominantly penitential in nature. There is a great stress on human sinfulness. Nobody will receive Communion without having confessed their sins to a priest the day or the hour before the celebration of the Eucharist. There is a great beauty to this spiritual vision because it shows God's splendor and grace in the face of human depravity. The people in the West have much to learn from their Eastern brothers and sisters. The awareness of human sinfulness is hardly existent in the West. Few people in the West appreciate the sacrament of reconciliation.

Participants at the retreats in Novyi Rozdil.

But on the other hand the gospel proclaims human freedom and human dignity, which is of great importance for a people trying to find their identity among the nations. It would be a great tragedy if the struggles for equal rights, good housing, good work, good medical care, good education, and the many facilities the West has to offer were to be perceived as contrary to the values of the gospel of Jesus Christ. It is precisely the gospel that proclaims the dignity of the human person and encourages us in the fight for justice and peace. Capitalism and communism both have failed to offer justice and peace in the world. My great hope is that the young people of Ukraine will be guided by the gospel as they make their decisions for their own and their nation's future.

Retreats in Novyi Rozdil. Borys Gudziak (in the center) helped as a translator.

During the afternoon session the dean of the area, Father Vasyl Hovhera, and his wife, Maria, came to the retreat. Also present were the priest of the local parish, Father Mykola Midjak, and his assistant priest. They invited us to come to the Sunday morning liturgy in their nearby church. These priests were very kind people, very open, very flexible, very trusting, and willing to help us in every possible way. Father Mykola urged me to give the homily. I accepted. "Speak as long as you want," he said. Realizing that an Eastern Rite Eucharistic liturgy on Sunday would normally last at least two hours, I told them I would keep my words to five minutes. I probably won't be able to keep it that short, certainly not when Borys has to translate every word!

Novyi Rozdil—Sunday, August 8, 1993

This morning, after breakfast, I gave a short talk about the disciplines of the spiritual life. Then we gathered in front of our dormitory to start the twenty- minute walk to St. Volodymyr's Church. It became like a procession, or a pilgrimage. For a while we sang Taizé songs in Ukrainian and then walked silently on the road and through the fields. After a few minutes' walk we could see the many gray high-rises of Novyi Rozdil. It was a somber, depressing view. Novyi Rozdil was built fifteen years ago during the Soviet regime. The only word for it is "ugly." It reminds me of some of the similar developments outside New York City, Amsterdam, Paris, Rome, and other cities: great clusters of drab-looking buildings with little balconies where people hang their laundry to dry.

After walking through the fields for a minute, we noticed the little church of St. Volodymyr. Surrounded by the somber high-rise buildings the little church looked friendly and inviting. When we had only five more minutes to go, Borys asked us all to form close lines again. Then Vasyl Slipak and Yurko Kolassa, the two cantors of our group, intoned a beautiful Ukrainian hymn. [Vasyl Slipak became a famous opera singer and lived in Paris, France. When the Russian aggression started in 2014, he became a volunteer and was killed by a sniper in 2016.] Walking up the little hill to the church we noticed that a few hundred people were standing there to welcome us. As we came close to them they joined us in our song.

The little church was extended by a large wooden barracks to hold the overflow of people. But even that wasn't enough: many people stood outside the church close to the entrances. While we walked to the altar in procession, a large choir standing on the balcony of the little church sang beautiful polyphonic hymns. In the sacristy, the priests, Vasyl, Mykola, and his assistant were waiting for me. They gave me a big, heavy black cassock to wear with a golden stole.

For Nathan and me, this was our first Greek Catholic liturgy in Ukraine. It was a profound experience of prayer and praise. The richly decorated church; the colorful, embroidered vestments of the priests; the hymns, antiphons, and prayers— all sung in rich harmony—the devout attention of the people; the solemn gestures of the priests; and most of all, the feeling that we were with fellow Christians who so warmly welcomed us in their community, all of this made it an unforgettable spiritual experience.

It was, of course, long—and it was hot. There were no chairs or pews. Two hours of standing is not easy for Western legs. The sacristan offered me a chair, and I sat down for a few moments, but nobody else could so I felt somewhat embarrassed sitting on a chair surrounded by standing people, many of whom looked a lot older than I.

After the reading of the Gospel story of Jesus walking on the restless waters and inviting Peter to do the same, I offered a few thoughts about keeping our eyes fixed on Jesus as we live in the midst of the storms of our century. I thanked the people there for their great faithfulness during hard times and tried to encourage them not to be afraid of the many changes ahead of them. Mostly I wanted to express my conviction that with a clear spiritual focus we won't drown in the fearful insecurities of our lives.

Fr. Henri preaches at the parish church in Novyi Rozdil.

At the moment of the Eucharistic prayer, Vasyl, the dean and main celebrant, motioned me to come to the altar and join him and the other priest in saying the prayers. While all the other priests sang their petitions, I recited a few of them in English, to which the choir responded in Ukrainian with, "Lord have mercy" and "Grant this, O Lord."

After the celebration, which lasted from 11:40 a.m. until 1:40 p.m., the pastor Mykola Midjak said a few heartfelt words to all of us who had come to join in the parish liturgy and thanked me for the words of encouragement.

It was a very profound event for all of us. The retreat became more than a retreat. It also became a form of proclamation. The faith and love of the young people who came to the retreat now became a sign of hope for the many people who lived in the depressing world of cement and sulfur factories.

As we walked back through the fields to the summer camp we all felt grateful to have been able to celebrate the Eucharist in such a festive as well as life-giving way.

This afternoon at 4 p.m. we concluded the retreat with a joyful celebration. After a few animated Taizé songs, many people spoke about the way the weekend had affected them. I was deeply moved by the great spiritual impact this short retreat had had on them. They spoke about new hope, new vision and new energy to continue their life.

At 5 p.m. the buses left—full of teary people. Vladzio drove us back to Lviv, and at 7 p.m. we were "home" again at the Dnister Hotel.

ᛟ

Lviv—Monday, August 9, 1993

Nathan and I didn't want to leave Ukraine without a visit to a psychiatric institution. We knew that in Ukraine people with mental handicaps and people with mental illness were living together in the same "hospitals," and we very much hoped that we could get a firsthand impression of such hospitals.

It wasn't easy to organize. Zenia had to go to the office of the president of the Lviv region, and get a letter from the vice-premier minister and the formal permission of the department that oversees the psychiatric institutions. It is clear that very few foreigners ask for such permission and that those who do ask are perceived more as inspectors than as people who have a personal interest in the "patients."

It took Zenia most of the morning to get the necessary papers, and at 2 p.m. Vladzio drove Nathan, Zenia, Mykola, and me to the village of Yaktoniv, a forty-five-minute drive from Lviv.

It wasn't easy to find the psychiatric institution. There were no signs pointing to it. After asking several people for directions, we saw a handicapped man wandering near a bus station and we assumed that we must be close to the institution. The man joined us in the van and showed us the side road that led us to the Hrushka Psychoneurological Institute, as it was officially called.

As we drove into the little compound we saw several men sitting in the grass or just standing about. They stared at us with empty eyes without moving or uttering a word. I sensed an atmosphere of hopelessness, despair, and resignation. These poorly dressed, isolated individuals just stood or sat, aimlessly waiting for nothing and nobody.

As we walked around searching for someone to give us permission to look at the place, a man in his fifties wearing blue jeans and a yellow shirt appeared and greeted us. His name was Yuriy Volodymyrovych Tymoshchuk. He was the director of the Hrushka Institute. Later we found out that he was a medical doctor who, after twenty-five years of medical service in the army, had accepted the task of fixing up and running the institute. As we walked around he said, "Administration is an easy thing for me. The army gave me good experience." Dr. Tymoshchuk was polite and friendly but formal and very cautious in his answers. It became clear that he wanted to give us a good impression. The bedrooms, recreation hall, and dining space he showed us looked clean and well-kept, but Zenia felt that a telephone call from the department of social services announcing our visit might have been the main reason that things looked relatively decent. This could have been true, because when we came to the rooms with severely handicapped men, we were shocked by their pitiful condition. They were laying in their beds, smelling badly and looking miserable in their dirty sheets. The isolation and aloneness of these men were very depressing. One older man sitting half-naked on the floor said only, "I want to go home, I want to go home."

Although there are fewer than one hundred residents in the place, the director didn't know their names. He was more eager to show us things than to introduce us to people.

He led us to a new, still unfinished building. "We hope to have no more than two patients in one room," he said, "but we have run out of money and don't know when we can finish this project." He also took us to the cow barn, a place for packaging glasswork, and the orchard. Meanwhile, we kept asking questions about the men we had seen. It was clear that the attention of the director was given mostly to buildings and facilities.

Nathan asked him several questions about the care for the residents and about their relationships with the staff and the people of the neighborhood. The doctor's answers made it clear that he envisioned a self-supporting institution with adequate facilities and minimum contact with the outside world. From our few conversations with the men, it seemed that most of them had lost their parents and that only a very few were receiving visits from relatives or friends.

Dr. Tymoshchuk told us, "When I came here one-and-a-half years ago, all residents were locked up. I changed that. Now most of them can freely walk around and be outside during the day. It has been a great change. We need much less medication than before." Nathan asked, "Can some of the men go into the village on their own?" "No, no," he replied. "Those who wander off by themselves, we keep locked up." He obviously had not been aware of the man we had picked up at the bus stop.

Walking through one of the dormitories we spoke a little with the women who worked there. Some of them had been at Hrushka for more than twenty years, but it didn't seem that they had developed intimate relationships with the men. "Look at him," one said. "He has a very smart brother—what a pity!"

The thought that these men have anything to offer—that they may even have a gift for society—seems completely absent. They were poor, pitiful men who were the sad victims of their birth trauma. The way they stood around, silently looking at us, made us feel as if we were in a prison camp for people who didn't deserve attention.

Fr. Henri, Nathan, and Zenia speak with the "patients" at Hrushka Psychoneurological Institute—an institution for mentally handicapped persons.

Zenia, in her wonderfully spontaneous way, walked up to several of the men, gently touched them, and spoke to them. Some of them smiled warmly at her, and those who could speak told her about the death of their parents and their hope for a visit from a sister or brother. I sat down with one of the men with Down syndrome. He smiled at me and put his head against my chest, grateful for a little attention and affection. Dr. Tymoshchuk said, "Not long ago people with Down syndrome didn't live longer than twenty years, but since all the changes we have made they can become as old as twenty-eight!" When he said this, Nathan and I looked at each other realizing that the members of Daybreak with Down syndrome are living into their fifties and sixties.

One question we asked the director was what he thought about men and women living together in the same institution. He said that it would not be a good idea because it would require much more staff. When we told him that in Canada, at some institutions, there was a problem of abuse of residents by staff members, he said, "That can't happen here because we have only women aides and they all have a very motherly attitude. They wouldn't abuse anybody."

At the entrance to one of the buildings stood a man in his forties, clinging to the railing of the stairs. Dr. Tymoshchuk said, "He came only a few months ago. When his parents died he lived among animals for a long time. He didn't speak and was very fearful when he came. Now he is saying a few words and he is gradually becoming able to walk on his own two feet." We tried to speak to him, but he hardly looked at us. It seemed as if he were living in another world.

As we said our goodbyes to the director, he said, "You should have come a few years later. Then this place will look a lot better. I am sorry that things are still in such a bad state today. But we are working to make it better."

Meanwhile, we kept thinking about the painful isolation of the residents. I found it very hard to leave without shaking hands with each of the men. They looked so lonely, so lost, so forgotten. They have a place, they have a bed, they have food. But do they have a friend? Are they even ever seen as human beings with a unique personality? Do they ever make a walk into town, go on a trip, meet people who want to welcome them into their homes? Do they ever feel truly loved?

Our visit may have been much too short to answer these questions, but the isolation not only of these men but also of the institution as a whole made us wonder how much "at home" these men will ever feel.

As we drove back to Lviv, I wondered whether it would be good for Dr. Tymoshchuk to come to Daybreak and live with us for a while. He obviously wanted to do the best he could within his own perspective. As a man who had lived for twenty-five years in the army, discovering the unique gifts of handicapped people is obviously not his primary concern. Buildings and facilities are. When I asked if he could consider coming to Toronto, he said, "When you invite me!" I wonder if we should.

Lviv—Tuesday, August 10, 1993

During the retreat, Theodore Gudziak and Lesia Kryp-iakevych, a cousin and friend of Borys, invited us to come to the office of the Youth for Christ organization. This organization grew out of a large youth rally that took place, on Borys's initiative, in Lviv in September 1990. On that occasion around forty thousand young people came together for various events to publicly manifest and celebrate their faith. It was the first time after the Soviet regime had collapsed that such a free expression of religion was possible. There was so much good energy at that rally in 1990 that the organizers decided to set up a permanent office to educate and form the thousands of young people who are hungry for spiritual nourishment.

At 2 p.m. we had lunch at the Youth for Christ office and discussed the possibility of developing a retreat ministry in Ukraine. Nathan, Borys, Zenia, and I had discussed at length how young men and women in Ukraine wanted the kind of experience we had offered during the weekend. It seemed that this was the opportune time to set up a ministry that would be able to reach out to Ukrainian youth. The Youth for Christ organization has facilities, people, money, space, and time to do it.

It meant a lot to Nathan and me that on our last day in Ukraine we had an opportunity to speak with people who had the capacity to continue some of the work we had done during our short stay. We hope that, in the year ahead, different members of the Daybreak community can come to Lviv to help in the development of this retreat ministry. The staff feels strongly that they can do much in terms of organization and planning but need continuing help in terms of content and inspiration.

Back at the Dnister Hotel, the dining hall manager gave us a special room for our last dinner in Lviv. It was good to be together, the four of us, in this quiet space and talk about the ten days we had spent together. We were full of gratitude and very happy that we had been able to live the week together. It will take each of us a while to fully appreciate all that we experienced, but all four of us knew already that this trip would have lasting consequences for our relationship with one another and with Ukraine.

Chobham—Wednesday, August 11, 1993

After celebrating the Eucharist in the hotel room, Vladzio, Mykola, and his daughter Mariana joined Zenia, Borys, Nathan, and me. At 10 p.m. we all drove to the Lviv airport.

As we entered the airport building we were surprised by a little choir singing the Taizé Magnificat for us. Six members of Faith and Light had come all the way to the airport to say thank-you and goodbye. The many people who crowded the place looked puzzled at the sound of this joyful song. I was deeply moved by this gesture of friendship. There were many handshakes, kisses, and tears—and wonderful farewell gifts. It was very hard for Nathan and me to take leave of Zenia and Borys. We had grown so close in the past few days. Suddenly it was over!

After going through customs and passport control, we kept waving at our friends from a distance, but then Nathan and I found ourselves alone together in the waiting room. Although the four of us had been able to express our gratitude to each other, and although we had shared with one another how each of us had experienced the ten days in Lviv, the separation still seemed very abrupt and radical. As Nathan and I sat in the restless waiting room wondering why it took so long to board the plane, we realized how handicapped we were without Zenia and Borys. Our five Ukrainian words didn't allow us to find out what was happening. But when we looked out of the window we realized that getting the luggage to the plane seemed to be the main problem.

Bidding farewell at Lviv airport. The young man squatting is
Vasyl Slipak, future opera singer, killed by a Russian sniper in 2016.

LOT Airlines took us from Lviv to Warsaw. From Warsaw we flew, via Krakow, to London. The move from Lviv to London was truly a move to the West. The Warsaw airport with its many duty-free shops full of luxury items was already a world away from Lviv, but the vibrant, intense life at Heathrow Airport in London nearly shocked us into the full awareness of how large the distance between East and West still is.

Back at Brookplace with Patricia and Bart, Nathan and I had a chance to tell our story. As I listened to Nathan's impressions, I realized that only by telling our stories can the countless impressions be sorted out. In the context of a familiar language, familiar people, and a familiar milieu, we can start to articulate what we had seen, heard, and felt. Probably, many long "stories" will be needed to get fully in touch with our Ukraine experience and to discover its long-term significance.

Rotterdam—Thursday, August 12, 1993

At 11 a.m. Nathan and I left Brookplace for Heathrow Airport. Ahead of Nathan was a seven-hour flight to Toronto; ahead of me, a hop over the English Channel to Rotterdam.

Nathan and I had taken an emotional risk in making the Ukrainian trip together. Our friendship during the last seven years has been intense and complex. Now we can both say that, whatever our Ukrainian trip had meant for each of us, it had definitely deepened our bond and strengthened our affection for each other. I will probably remember our journey as much for the deep experience of friendship as for the experience of a new country. My strong desire for affection and intimacy makes me a needy travel companion. Nathan's need for privacy makes him seem aloof and distant. But during this trip we could respect each other's needs and feel close without clinging, and separate without feeling rejected.

We are gradually discovering the disciplines of friendship. When Nathan is quiet and pensive, I have to learn that this doesn't mean that he is fed up with me. When I am asking for attention and a little special time to be together, Nathan has to learn that this does not mean that I want to possess him. These are certainly not easy disciplines since our spontaneous reactions are to feel rejected or to feel invaded. But these days were very good for us, and I trust that our deepened mutual love will bear many fruits in our life at Daybreak. A very old truth was confirmed: friendship can grow deep and strong when based on a common concern. Ukraine and our bonds with Zenia and Borys had created the space for us to be well together and see clearer each other's unique gifts. Not by looking at each other but by looking together at the needs of others did we come to the realization of how important we are for each other.

Surrounded by thousands of people waiting for planes taking them to the ends of the earth, we embraced each other, grateful that Zenia and Borys's invitation to see their country had opened in us a new desire to live our lives at Daybreak with new trust and new confidence.

Rotterdam—Friday, August 13, 1993

My brother Paul and I were both invited to attend the opening of an icon exhibition and sale in Huis ter Duin, a large seaside luxury hotel in the summer resort known as Nordwjk aan Zee.

As we drove to the hotel, Paul told me about his trip to Ghana from which he had just returned. He said, "I have never seen such misery. There are large slums where people live in the most horrendous conditions. The streets are lined with thousands of people trying to sell a few fruits or vegetables. You wonder how people survive in such abject poverty. And still … the atmosphere is not depressing. People smile at you, kids play freely, and wherever you go you are received with great friendliness and kindness. Notwithstanding the countless shacks and overcrowded huts, the lack of food and health care, the people of Ghana seem to be a happy people."

As Paul was speaking it suddenly became clear what a completely different impression Ukraine had made on me. I had not seen any slums there, nor people living in huts or shacks. I hadn't seen abject poverty or great misery. What I had seen was a country where everyone—young and old, teachers and students, shopkeepers and businesspeople—were poor compared with the standard of living in Holland or England, but nobody was without the basic necessities of life. People earn very little, but practically everyone has some sort of a job. But what I had also seen was a people without smiles. I hadn't seen children playing in the streets, nor heard any joyful sounds. I had seen a country with sad faces, little interpersonal contact, and a somber mood.

Ukraine is very different from Ghana, very different too from Bolivia, Peru, or any of the Latin American countries I have visited. In Ukraine, everyone is able to live, but few are living with joy. There is no great separation between the wealthy and the poor as in many Third World countries. There are no "young towns" as in Lima, nor "favelas" as in São Paolo. There are no overcrowded streets as in Mexico City, nor large areas without water or light as in Honduras or Haiti. But there is a large, seemingly impenetrable cloud of somberness covering everyone.

What about the future of Ukraine? The Soviet oppression has come to an end, but will the West bring a higher standard of living for the people? With the rapid rise of inflation as well as unemployment, it is quite likely that soon Ukraine will see a few become rich, and many becoming miserable. Will Ukraine become a Third World country like Ghana?

And what about joy? The centuries-long suffering of the Ukrainian people combined with their melancholy temperament does not make it likely that the Ukrainian people will soon become a "happy people." They never expected much happiness in this life. Their beautiful liturgies on Sundays and Feast days are the places where they catch a glimpse of the heavenly kingdom, but only a glimpse. Life for the Ukrainian people is lived, mostly, as a long—very long—journey to the promised land: a land that remains far, far away.

When Paul and I arrived at the Huis ter Duin Hotel and were escorted by our hosts to the icon exhibition, I was quite overwhelmed by the irony of the situation. Here I was shown splendid icons coming from the churches in Russia, Ukraine, Greece, Bulgaria, and other Eastern countries. They were painted with great devotion, to be venerated in the sacred liturgy. I had not seen such beautiful icons in Ukraine. Most of the art I saw in the churches there was quite tasteless and often imitations of eighteenth-century European devotional pictures. But in this luxurious hotel, I could see the splendor of the Eastern Church and even buy it! Most of these icons had come to the West during the Soviet years.

When I looked at the prices of the icons I realized that each one of them would be sold for more money than most Ukrainians will earn during their whole life. And where would these icons finally end up? Not in the churches for which they were made, but in the homes of art-loving Dutch families.

After some hesitation, I decided to buy myself one of the icons for the chapel at Daybreak. It is a splendid Ukrainian icon of the Virgin with Three Hands. Maybe one day I will return it. It would mean a lot to me if Zenia and Borys could see it come home and become part of their prayer with handicapped people.

🔱

Rotterdam—Saturday, August 14, 1993

On July 24 I began this Ukraine diary. Today I want to conclude it. The question for me now is, what will be the long-term fruits of this journey?

Before I went I had the feeling that something significant would happen, something that would have a deep effect on my life and the lives of my friends. Did something like that happen? Zenia has returned to her work for Faith and Light and is going again from place to place to create communities of care among people with handicapped children. Borys has returned to his work at the historical institute. Nathan, after a few days of rest in Canada, will return to Daybreak and continue his work as director of the community, and I will fly back to Canada within two weeks, facing a full schedule of pastoral work in the community and lectures and retreats all over the United States and Canada.

How can we hold on to the spirit of our Ukrainian experience, a spirit of friendship and common care?

I am deeply convinced that what we lived together has the potential of great fruitfulness. But there will be no fruits without pruning the tree! It will require some real discipline not to get so busy again with the many ups and downs of daily life that the Ukrainian experience soon becomes a vague memory.

Still, it is not easy to know how to go from here. There is the proposal to develop a nationwide retreat ministry in which

Ukrainian Youth for Christ and Daybreak will work closely together. There is the plan of Zenia and Borys to come on a regular basis to Canada to strengthen and deepen the bonds that grew during this trip and to explore new ways of working together for Ukraine. There is the desire to get a typewriter and electric wheelchair for Andriy and a large supply of diapers for Taras and his brother. All or some of this will certainly happen. But most important, it seems to me, is that many people in Daybreak and many people in Ukraine will discover that they are brothers and sisters and that the distance caused by the evil powers of war, exploitation, and oppression will become less and less, and that a sense of solidarity, yes even community, can grow that transcends the many people-made boundaries.

More than ever, I believe in the gift of handicapped people to create such a community. Their weakness is God's strength; their dependence is God's invitation to create bonds of love and support; their poverty is God's way to bring us the blessings of the Kingdom. The handicapped men and women from Canada, Ukraine, and all countries in the world, whether in the East or in the West, call us through their common poverty to build a Kingdom of peace and love that has no boundaries but is a sign of hope for a world that yearns for freedom.

PART TWO

Friday, August 5, 1994—Sunday, August 21, 1994

A year after their first visit, Henri Nouwen and Nathan Ball went to Ukraine again, hoping to establish a lasting bond between L'Arche Daybreak in Toronto and the Faith and Light community in Lviv. They now had invited three other members of the Daybreak community to join them: Sister Sue Mosteller, Cheryl Zinyk, and Siobhan Keogh. Sue, a longtime member of Daybreak, was a close friend of Zenia Kushpeta. Cheryl, who had joined Daybreak as an assistant in 1992, had Ukrainian grandparents and was excited to visit her ancestral homeland for the first time. Siobhan Keogh was a former Daybreak assistant and friend of Zenia's. She had flown out to Lviv ahead of the others to help Zenia with preparations for the visit and to acquaint herself with Ukraine.

The group flew from Toronto on Friday, August 5, 1994, landing the next day in Warsaw. Borys Gudziak, flying from Boston, missed his connection due to bad weather and joined the group in Warsaw on Sunday, August 7.

In Warsaw, they were picked up in the early morning by
Lubomyr Boyanivisky and Hryhoriy Ivaniukh from Lviv, who
had just driven eight hours through the night from Ukraine to
Poland. Both drivers were experienced at crossing borders, as
Henri's account attests.

About a half hour before we came to the border, Hryhoriy
parked the car on the roadside. Lubomyr got out with a plastic
bag, pulled out a long black cassock, and put it on. "What is
this about?" we asked. "Oh, he got a cassock from the Studite
sisters," Borys said. "With a 'priest' we will get through the
border faster!"

Lubomyr showed us a formal letter from Cardinal
Lubachivsky, the head of the Ukrainian Greek Catholic
Church, in which he addressed the border police asking them
please to let "Henri Nouwen and his delegation" pass the
border quickly.

We knew that it could take as long as four hours to get
through all of the Polish and Ukrainian passport and custom
controls. With the cassock and the letter, Lubomyr hoped to
receive special attention from the customs officers! It was quite
a piece of theatre. When we came to the border, Lubomyr, who
now looked like a pale young seminarian in a much-too-large
cassock, walked to the uniformed border gatekeeper holding
in one hand the large envelope containing the cardinal's letter
and a rosary in the other. He unfolded the letter and began to
read it aloud. He assumed that the Polish guy wouldn't be able

to read Ukrainian. It seemed to work. It took only thirty-five minutes to jump through all the hoops. Many serious-looking Polish and Ukrainian policemen, endless stamping of pieces of paper and passports, and repeated inspections of the cardinal's letter finally got us into Ukraine.

"Why is it all so complicated?" we wondered. "Leftover bureaucracy from the Soviet time," Borys said. None of this is necessary but they have gotten used to it, and it will take a while to make it simpler. Moreover, the Poles and the Ukrainians are not eager to make it easy for each other. As we crossed the border, Borys showed us the old barbed-wire fences and lookout towers meant to keep people from escaping during the Soviet era.

As we drove into Ukraine, Cheryl was clearly excited. She was the first of her family to reenter their country of origin. "Welcome to your country," we said.

At 7 p.m. we arrived at the Dnister Hotel in Lviv, where we had stayed during our last visit. Zenia was waiting for us outside with a large bouquet of flowers. She was radiant and truly happy to see us. We all received a few flowers and many hugs. Ivanka and her son were also there to welcome us. The hotel and its surroundings looked very familiar to Nathan and me. Nothing had changed since last year.

"Get yourselves settled," Zenia said. "In half an hour we will go to my apartment to have dinner and a birthday celebration for Siobhan." Siobhan Keogh, a past assistant and a close friend of the Daybreak community, had come to Lviv a few weeks earlier to support Zenia in her work and to get a firsthand experience of the Ukrainian situation. She had first visited the L'Arche community in Budapest and then made her way by train to Lviv. In the short time she had been here she had made many friends, seen many places, and learned many Ukrainian words.

The party was a happy reunion. Mykola, his daughter Mariana, and his son Andriiko were there. Andriiko had grown visibly. As a six-year-old he was a lot harder to carry. I held him for a while in my lap, and he smiled generously at me. Mykola said proudly, "He is doing a lot better. He is now able to keep his head up."

Vladzio Pomisko, our driver from last year, also joined us. He looked well and quite happy. We made two new friends, Oleh and Oksana. Oleh is a medical student from Lviv, who just spent a few months with L'Arche in Trosly, France, and has become one of the leaders of the Faith and Light youth group that meets every Wednesday night. Oksana Kunanec is a physiotherapist from Toronto who came to her country of origin after working in Armenia and plans to work here for the near future with people with handicaps.

It was a joyful celebration, but after an hour, my fatigue became close to exhaustion, and I lay down on the large bed beside little Andriyko and fell into a deep sleep until Vladzio drove us to the Dnister Hotel in the newly furnished van.

Monday, August 8, 1994

Things have not become better in Ukraine since last year. For most people in Lviv the election of Leonid Kuchma as president was a major setback. Kuchma plans to create closer economic ties with Russia, and the people in western Ukraine have a deep fear of losing their independence and becoming subject again to Russian domination. Although most western Ukrainians have a strong view about the national identity of a united Ukraine embracing west as well as east (Lviv as well as Kyiv), there are also voices in the west to separate east from west and seek independence for the west alone. So many Russians are in fact living within the boundaries of eastern Ukraine that complete independence from Moscow seems to be an unrealistic expectation.

As we drove into Lviv yesterday, Borys pointed out that privatization of the farms had scarcely taken place. In fact, the recent local elections had given power back to the bosses of the old regime, so true democratization seemed a faraway dream. The democratic political powers were so poorly organized and had so little experience that the former rulers easily regained their influence. The few who tried to start farming on their own found themselves faced with endless obstacles.

For the first few years after the independence of Ukraine, people lived with expectations of greater freedom and prosperity. Now a period of disillusionment has set in. For many people life has become harder instead of easier. Runaway inflation, the lack of political leadership, the lack of support from the West, and the increasing influence of organized crime on all levels of the economy have created a deep sense of failure and even despair.

It became clear to us that our task of offering a little hope would be very hard to fulfill during our two weeks in Ukraine. There is little ground for optimism. There are no people or events to point to that allow us to suggest that things will be any better soon. It is much more likely that they will be worse. What, then, is the good news we have to proclaim? It is the news that we do not belong to this world and that only by claiming that truth can we live in it.

For outsiders like us, it is easy to see that the great temptation is to become bitter, angry, and resentful, because of the countless disillusionments and betrayals. Thus, we allow the darkness to overcome the light and we end up adding to the darkness ourselves.

During lunch in the hotel, Theodore, Borys's cousin, joined us to discuss the program for our stay. It looks quite full. As we thought about themes and titles for the lectures and retreats we were supposed to give, we soon ran into problems of language. Titles such as "Claiming Your Belovedness," "Living Our Life with Hope, Courage, and Confidence," "Being Called to Leadership," and so forth seem untranslatable. All these somewhat empowering titles had no equivalent in the spiritual language of Ukraine and easily sounded too arrogant or political, or simply too "foreign."

Borys Gudziak explains some facts about Ukrainian history in the local park, as Sister Sue Mosteller, Cheryl (standing), and Henri listen.

As I listened to the conversations about subject matter, I realized again how "Western" my spiritual thinking is and how important it is for me to stay close to the truth that the spirituality of Eastern Christianity is marked by long-suffering. The people who have experienced so few victories in the secular domain have come to see the Christian faith as a call to follow the crucified Christ as the way to a joy and peace that cannot be reached in this world.

For me, *hope* is a virtue that is not simply based on an "afterlife" but that directly affects my sense of being here and now. For me, hope, although reaching beyond the present moment, allows me to live in the present moment with courage and confidence. But for the people in Ukraine, the present is primarily a prison to escape from, a trap to get out of, or an experience to suffer through as best as one can.

So how does one bring hope to people who don't see any promise in the moment they are living through? I don't want to sound like a naive "positive thinker" from the wealthy West, but I also don't want to proclaim a gospel that builds all expectations on a life with Christ in heaven. One thing is clear to me. We have to let people know that we do our utmost to understand their unique situation and base our words of hope on that understanding.

At 4 p.m. we all gathered in the park in front of the hotel to listen to Borys, who would give us a short overview of the complicated Ukrainian history. What struck me most in reviewing this history was that independence is a new concept for Ukraine. Except for the two years of failed independence in the post–World War I years, Ukraine has in modern times never experienced a clear national identity. Even today there are many discussions about the nature of the Ukrainian state. Is it a political, an ethnic, or a territorial unity? Is there enough basis on which to build a state? Many Russians consider present-day Ukraine as a totally artificial entity. Is there enough inner cohesion to keep together a nation that has little experience of statehood and that includes a 25 percent minority population? Or is it doomed to be torn apart constantly by inner strife and outer aggression? At present there is a lot of anxiety around these questions.

At 6:30 we all came together to celebrate the Eucharist: Sue, Cheryl, Zenia, Nathan, Siobhan, Borys, and I. After the readings we each expressed how we felt. There were many tears and many smiles. It seemed most important that we, as a small Christian community, would live these coming days with special attentiveness to one another and a strong commitment to live this "mission" together. Personally I realized that it wouldn't be easy to live as united as we had last year. Being a larger group, we will have to work harder than ever to be a community that witnesses as one body. The simple fact that each person has his or her own idea about how things need to be done asks for much time and energy. But it is a good challenge. It is the challenge that comes with growth.

Tuesday, August 9, 1994

We spent most of the day at the hotel talking and preparing for the days to come. At 4 p.m. Borys gave us a talk about the vision of the two great church leaders, Sheptytsky and Slipyj, concerning the ecclesiastical identity of the Greek Catholic Church. Although Nathan and I had heard most of the facts last year, it was a vivid reminder to me of the importance of charismatic leadership in the church. What most struck me was the way Slipyj, after his release from the labor camps and his expulsion from the Soviet Union, went from country to country visiting Ukrainian-Catholic communities, building a sense of belonging to a church within the Catholic communion. He stressed in word and action that Ukrainian Greek Catholics are not simply Roman Catholics who use a different rite, but are a church with its own synod, its own spirituality, and its own charism. As a church, the Greek Catholics have their own unique contribution to make in the larger family of the Catholic communion.

Slipyj's strong, charismatic personality lies at the origin of Borys's vocation. Borys said, "Meeting Slipyj on his visits to the United States in 1968 and 1976 made me desire to get through college and go to Rome to study in the presence of this deeply committed spiritual leader."

Where are the spiritual leaders in the Church today? Who are the people who can make true disciples who want to "lay down their lives for their friends" and work for the renewal of the Church and society? More important questions may be, Do I have the courage to call people to a radical service to Jesus and the Church? Do I dare to give leadership, even when that leadership requires me to make unpopular choices? The story of Slipyj, who dared to be unpopular to realize his vision, raises some hard questions for me.

Wednesday, August 10, 1994

The Faith and Light communities—including parents, their children with handicaps, and friends—welcomed us warmly with songs, flowers, and the traditional offering of bread and salt. We all gathered in the children's library building close to the church of Volodymyr and Olha, where Nathan and I were first welcomed last August.

Zenia had organized this day of prayer and celebration for the three little communities she had founded since her arrival in Lviv more than two years ago. Until now they had come together for evenings, afternoons, and even for camps, but this was the first full day of retreat for Faith and Light. Many of the people whom Nathan and I met last year in their homes were there. There were also many new faces. Altogether there were about sixty people.

Looking at the gray, somber building surrounding us, and the somber-looking people crossing the streets, this little community of marginal people looked like a little light in the darkness. The songs, the clapping of hands, most of all the many smiles made this gathering of poor people look like God's chosen ones on the road to the promised land.

Beneath all the smiles and warm words there was much suffering, much frustration, and disillusionment. After all, the past year had not made life any easier, and all these people were still caught in a society that simply lacks the most basic structures for service, communication, and transportation. We got a very real taste of that when, during an unsupervised moment, Halyna, a young girl in our group, ran off by herself. "Where is Halyna?" people asked. She was nowhere to be found. After an hour of looking through all the surrounding streets and alleyways, someone went to a nearby police station. There they simply said, "We only start looking for lost people after they have been lost for three days!" Halyna, who cannot speak and walks with difficulty, would not be able to find her way by herself. She could have boarded any bus and gone anyplace. There was no one to call or warn. It suddenly hit me how completely unprotected people with handicaps are in this milieu. After an hour of searching in all directions, one of the group leaders found her near a neighborhood store and brought her back. When she returned, everyone in the group spontaneously started singing, "Alleluia, alleluia," while dancing in little groups of two and three. Halyna just enjoyed the little party for her. She did not seem to have been worried about much!

This incident shows how close joy and sorrow are. In the midst of all the singing and dancing, one person is missing, and people feel fear in their hearts. In the midst of all the disappointments and personal pain, beautiful harmonies emerge. The poor offer their blessings, but the blessings often reveal how poor they are!

Zenia led the day with her exuberant spirit, Sue and I both gave a reflection, Cheryl offered guidance to the small groups and helped people make large banners with the history of Faith and Light. Siobhan choreographed a dance with the wheelchairs, and many people prepared sandwiches, arranged flowers, presented a skit, helped with name tags, and were active with one thing or another. It seemed that everyone was a leader and everyone a follower.

At noon, Zenia, Sue, Nathan, and I met with the parents. Each parent spoke for a few minutes. There was an abundant expression of gratitude. Many said, "Here in Faith and Light, my child is happy. Here my child feels loved and is valued, here my child laughs and plays. At home, isolated in our apartment, my child can be very restless, anxious and unruly, but here my child is different." Everybody tried very hard to be positive and express gratitude, but it didn't take many words to talk about the great suffering that is close to the surface and won't easily go away. There are problems with transportation and medical care. There are complaints about getting on a bus, being accepted in schools, and not having ramps for wheelchairs.

It became clear to me how isolated most of these parents felt. Many of them had no spouse and very little help on a day-to-day basis. Faith and Light offered moral and emotional support, but many basic necessities were still lacking. I realized that I should not be too fast in calling people to joy, peace, and gratitude. Important as that is, many parents need a space to express their accumulated feelings of frustration, disappointment, anger, resentment, and deep physical and emotional fatigue. They need to be heard with a heart that wants to understand, and with a mind that looks for ways to make their lives a little easier. Sometimes a new wheelchair, a typewriter, a new ramp, or a regular visitor can make all the difference.

At the end of the day we walked in procession to the nearby church. There we gathered around the little altar. One of the young assistants read a hymn written especially for Faith and Light by Andriy, our poet friend. Father Petro Harasymchuk, who had been with us the whole day, said, "These people ask me to do things I do not like to do, but I know that here in real life I am growing." After his words, he gave us the final blessing. When we had returned to the hotel, our small team celebrated the Eucharist. It was the Feast of St. Lawrence, and the readings spoke about giving freely without compulsion, and about gaining life by losing it. They invited us to look in a new way at all that we had seen and experienced this day. We saw much selfless generosity, but also much losing of life. It is not easy to trust that all of this will bear fruit somehow, somewhere.

Thursday, August 11, 1994

This morning we spent time at Borys's Institute of Church History and at the Svichado publishing company. In the afternoon, we gave a press conference at the Building of Solemn Events (the Potocki Palace). We also listened to a talk by Borys about the Orthodox Church in Ukraine, celebrated the Eucharist in Sue's hotel room, had a long dinner, took a short walk through the park, and talked about the coming retreat.

At the historical institute as well as at the publishing company, there was a great desire for the staff to have experience outside of Ukraine. Oksana, Natalia, and Donata, three members of the Institute of Church History staff, had just returned from a three- to five-month stay in the United States. They learned English and computer skills and, most of all, got a very different notion about ways to run an office, all in the context of experiencing different models of church.

Yet not everything that is possible in the United States, however, can be simply applied in Ukraine. One of the harsh realities of Ukraine is that personal and professional needs constantly intersect. In order to get food, you have to stand in line for many hours. Work has to be interrupted constantly to fulfill basic personal and family needs. Sometimes one secretary will leave the office for a few hours to do the shopping for the whole staff. Then there are all the problems with office space, telephone lines, computer parts, transportation, and all the other services needed to make an office run smoothly.

At the publisher's office, a staff of people was packed into four small rooms, doing all the acquisition of new titles, the editing, marketing, and distributing. There is a great commitment to religious publishing, and since we last met, nearly twenty new books have been published, mostly translations from English, French, or German.

Also in publishing, there is a need for a broader vision and more experience. Bohdan Trojanowski, the director of Svichado (The mirror), hopes to come to the United States to study English and visit several publishing companies to get new ideas and to learn new ways of publishing.

Much of the problem is financial. There is no money to license copyrights, to pay translators and printers, and to advertise well. Moreover, although Ukrainians are avid book readers, the readership for theological books is still limited, and few people can afford to buy books. With the bankruptcy of the state publishing monopoly, there is at present no distribution network. At the present time, there are very few Ukrainian spiritual authors, and the dependence on the West is still very real.

Visiting these offices and talking to these idealistic people, I keep wanting to jump in and make things happen faster, more efficiently, and with more results. As I suggest this or that, they often look at me as if I were pitifully naive and have little, if any, idea about how things work here. I think, *Well, we could make a list of significant spiritual books published in the United States, ask their publishers for free copyrights, and even create a special fund for religious publishing in Ukraine. Then we might gather some good translations, and give them some guidance*

about the usage of religious language in different cultures, set up
some large retreats where new books can be presented, and build a
volunteer team of people who work on distribution.

But I had better keep my mouth shut because all this naive
enthusiasm may only create the image of the "ugly American"
who wants to tell others how to do it his way. The way Bohdan
and his people do their work is probably a lot saner than
the way of many large American companies. Every week the
team meets not only to talk about their work but also about
their relationship with one another and with God. They are
true "amateurs," lovers, people who do not work for money or
success but for the spiritual well-being of the Ukrainian people.
Quite a few of them could have chosen to work in another
country for more money and with better facilities, but they
realized that Ukraine needs much spiritual support and that
they can offer it through their publications.

The press conference had a somewhat eerie quality.
Nathan, Sue, Cheryl, Borys, Zenia, and I were sitting on red
chairs on a podium in one of the large, empty palace rooms.
In front of us, ten people representing different newspapers
and radio and television stations were looking at us. Behind
them a few more were moving back and forth with cameras.
It was a rather flat event. We all made a little presentation
about who we were, why we had come to Lviv, and what we
planned to do here, and they asked a few questions about the
nature of a retreat, the ecumenical aspect of our lives, and
about our day-to-day relationships with people who have a
mental handicap. Most of the journalists didn't seem very

excited about much of our work and certainly didn't ask any challenging questions. When we left, Nathan said, "Well, we certainly talked a lot more than they did. It seemed more like a lecture than a press conference."

One question, however, stuck with us. The editor of the new bimonthly magazine of Youth for Christ asked, "Would you ever consider giving a retreat to journalists?" I often thought about that, since I have noticed frequently that those who write about religious affairs normally have very little religious formation themselves. This is even more the case in the United States and Western Europe than in Ukraine. Religious journalism can be a real ministry. More people are influenced by newspapers, magazines, and radio than by sermons from the pulpit. Still, few of the media people conceive of their work as a vocation to bring good news to their viewers, listeners, and readers. I would love to participate in some project that is geared to the spiritual formation of those who give their time and energy to religious reporting.

During the Eucharist we spoke about the importance of remaining close to each other during the coming days, when we are surrounded by the many people who will come to the retreat and the workshop. We all will be very busy, and the danger is that we will have little time for each other. Still, the most powerful witness will come from the way we work and live together as members of a community.

Friday, August 12, 1994

This morning, Sue, Cheryl, and Zenia went to visit Ivanka, her son, Oleh, and her brother Myron, and also Andriy and his mother who live on the same street. Nathan and I stayed at the hotel, writing and talking. After lunch, with Borys as our guide, we all made a little trip in the van to some of the most important churches of Lviv. All of these buildings and places made the complex history of the churches in Ukraine come alive. Often Borys said, "You remember when I talked about.... Well, it happened here." I was most moved when Borys pointed to the pulpit of the Transfiguration Church and said, "Here I preached at Easter 1990 for hundreds of young people about the face of Christ. It was that event that inspired us to organize the huge youth rally that was the beginning of the Youth for Christ movement in Ukraine."

Churches remind us of deep piety as well as painful divisions, of humble service as well as lust for power, of a sense of victory as well as the experience of defeat, of excellent leadership as well as vicious manipulation.

If stones could speak, they would speak about splendid liturgies and atrocious persecution, about reconciliation and hatred between religious groups, about self-giving and self-serving leadership, and about the divine as well as the demonic realities of church life. It seems that being in the world without being of it is less of a challenge than to be in the church without being of it!

At 4:30 p.m. a Volkswagen bus picked up Nathan, Sue, Cheryl, Siobhan, Zenia, and myself to bring us to Camp Rovesnyk, near the town of Chervonohrad, about two hours' drive from Lviv. The retreat and workshop will take place there.

How to describe Rovesnyk? We got there in pouring rain. It was very hard to find the place, but after asking many times, we got to a little building in the midst of the forest, and a dull-looking man in a gray suit and a gray tie told us that this was the place in which we were going to spend the weekend. After some waiting, we found our rooms, but not the normal things one expects: towels, drinking water, toilet paper, working lights, etc. Someone told us that the camp was built as a summer place for well-to-do Soviet officials, but it looked more like an unkempt camp for people condemned to forced labor. Soon we realized that there were about fifty rooms fewer than we needed, and that people who were supposed to be staying together were put far apart. Many who might have hoped for a room would have to sleep on the mattresses spread out in the gymnasium where our retreat sessions and liturgies were planned. Well, it seemed that everything that could go wrong did go wrong, and that everything you would have liked for your weekend holiday was missing.

Still, nobody seemed to worry too much. Even Zenia kept her cool and kept saying, "Oh, everything will be wonderful, everything will be fabulous." Within an hour after we arrived, 250 retreatants appeared, and for a while it was pure chaos. Naturally, there were a few complaints, but most people were just happy to be here and to be together. It took a few hours to sort it all out, and then we all had a "supper snack" in a room that holds about fifty people. Everyone got a hard-boiled egg and a slice of bread with margarine, a piece of tomato, and a glass of lukewarm tea.

Around 10:30 p.m. everyone gathered in the large gym for the opening session. There were introductions, songs, prayers, and short talks by Sue and myself about the story of Jesus and Peter walking on the water. At the end, Cheryl and Siobhan had created human waves among some of the participants: waves of loneliness, anger, oppression, victimization, abandonment, and despair. Everyone cried, "Lord save me," as a new wave rolled back and Jesus reached out his hand. All of this was to set the theme for the retreat: finding strength in Jesus as we walk on the waves of our restless lives.

By midnight all these many people had become a joyful gathering of Christians who were grateful to be together, with Jesus in the center. The final Eastern-Rite Vespers was a beautiful expression of unity and community.

As I looked at the students, the young professionals, and the mothers and their children with mental handicaps, and saw them all sitting on their mattresses in the gymnasium, I realized that joy and material comfort need not always go together.

It was after 1 a.m. when we finally made it to our beds. Exhausted, a little overwhelmed, but basically quite happy to be able to live all of this together in Ukraine.

Saturday, August 13, 1994

It is not easy to make an ugly-looking Soviet-built gymnasium—with one bench, two chairs, and two hundred mattresses covering most of the hard floor—look like a Greek Catholic church. Still, with a banner of Our Lady hanging from the basketball net, and a big plank put on a small table and a few candles here and there, we celebrated the Eucharist. While two priests co-celebrated, a third was hearing confessions. What made it a church, as always, were not the objects but the people. Amid all the mattresses where people had spent the night, all retreatants sang the Holy Eucharist together.

In the morning, I spoke about claiming our identity as the beloved daughters and sons of God, and in the afternoon, Sue spoke about community as the place of forgiveness and celebration. Cheryl led beautiful prayer responses, Siobhan led a dance, and Zenia, the singing. People were very present to it all and extremely attentive.

After the first talk, Zenia, Nathan, Sue, Cheryl, and I had a little session with the three Greek Catholic priests who were attending the conference: Father Petro, Father Ed, and Father Vlodymyr. We asked them how they were experiencing the conference, what their hopes were for their pastoral ministries, and how much personal support they received. It was a good meeting. Since we could not find a room to meet in, we sat on the stone steps in the hallway and a wooden bench that we had carried out of the conference room.

*Retreats at Rovesnyk camp. Fr. Henri talks with Maria
and her son Vadyk. and Mykola and his son Andriy.*

They all responded warmly to the conference but also expressed the need for more training in giving conferences such as this. They all felt the need for more youth ministry but complained that the ritualistic and legalistic older women in the church made it hard on young people to feel truly welcome. They all were happy to work in the church, but confessed that there were many conflicts among the clergy, and that not every bishop was supportive.

Father Ed Young is a special person. Born and raised in Brooklyn, New York, he had no ethnic connection with the Ukrainian Church. From his youth, however, he had experienced a call to serve the Eastern Church, inspired by Our Lady of Fatima, who had called the child visionaries to pray for the conversion of "Russia." He studied in Rome, worked for many years as a priest in the Greek Catholic church in the Stamford, Connecticut, Diocese, and recently had come to Lviv to work as dean of students in the seminary.

The stories he shared were quite startling. Until the end of the Soviet regime, there was no Catholic seminary in Lviv. Now, a few years later, there is a seminary, housed in a former youth camp with 300 men between the ages of seventeen and twenty-five. This year alone there were 250 applicants for the seminary. There were, however, only 60 places. The logistical problems are enormous. Having beds, providing food, and finding books were just a few. Many of the seminarians were sorely missed at home. Sometimes their mothers were widows, and the sons were needed to help kill the pig, dig potatoes, or harvest the crop. The bishop complained that seminarians were often gone from the seminary for long weekends or even whole months to work on their farms, but they had little choice: "If you have to go home to kill the pig, go home and kill the pig," Father Ed told them.

Father Ed had few illusions about motivation. "Becoming a priest is a big step up on the social ladder, and for many boys the priesthood is their way out of economic misery. Moreover they all will easily find good women to marry, since a priest is a good catch for Ukrainian women."

"How do they find a wife while in the seminary?" I asked.

"That is really no problem," Father Ed said. "They have long vacations, and many marriages are still arranged by the family. Before ordination they all get married. Sometimes it all happens within a few months at the end of their formal education."

Scenes from the retreats in Rovesnyk camp. Above, participants sit on the gym floor, disregarding their discomfort. Maria Savchuk and her son Vadyk are in the center. Sisters Uliana and Ira Kudla together with their mother Maria sit on both sides.

Fr. Henri preaches the retreats. Sister Sue Mosteller sits on his left.
Orysia during the retreats in Novyi Rozdil (August 1993).

Realism and idealism went hand in hand. Father Ed has given his life for the Church in Ukraine, but he was quite realistic about goals, aspirations, and motivation. At one point he quoted an Italian saying: "When there is no bread, there are many priests and many monasteries." Not everything that looks religious is religious, not everything that looks spiritual is spiritual, not everything that looks unselfish is unselfish. We all know it, but we are reminded of that in new ways when we step from our own world into another.

We concluded the day with a beautifully sung Vespers, followed by a long, silent prayer around the icon. The large space was lit by many small candles, and periods of silence were punctuated by Taizé melodies with Ukrainian words. It was a very intimate and sacred time. Solitude blended with community, community with solitude.

Sunday, August 14, 1994

At 10 a.m. all 250 of us gathered in the gymnasium and walked from there in procession through the woods to the little chapel at the entrance to the camp. As we walked we sang Eastern liturgical melodies and Western Taizé songs with Ukrainian words.

The chapel was a tiny little structure in the woods, just large enough for the sanctuary, where the priests conduct the liturgy. Outside was a little brick platform where people could attend the ceremonies. Father Ed was the main celebrant, and Father Petro, the co-celebrant. Just before the reading, the acolyte brought me a cassock and stole so that I too could enter the sanctuary as co-celebrant.

People sang with great conviction and piety, standing outside the little chapel. At least sixty children with their parents and friends, who stayed at the camp, joined us halfway through. After the Gospel reading about the multiplication of loaves and fishes, I gave a little homily saying that the love, friendship, kindness, and community we had experienced at the retreat might not feel like much, but that it would multiply when we give it away as Jesus gave away the bread and fish that *he* had received.

Fr. Henri preaches to the children during the retreats in Rovesnyk camp.

At the end of the liturgy, I said a few words and gave a special blessing to the children from Lviv and Kyiv who had joined us. It was a simple but very prayerful liturgy. Later Sue questioned what I had been doing during the long Communion time. "I suspect that there was a chair inside that little chapel and that you were sitting down while we had to stand outside. I don't think that's fair!" People in the East stand many hours: standing in line in front of a store, standing at bus stops or train stations, standing in the hours-long liturgies. Our Western legs are certainly not trained for so much standing!

At 2:30 we all came together again in the gymnasium for the final sessions and closing celebration. There was a beautiful mime about letting our hearts of stone become hearts of flesh. Sue and I spoke about the call to care for one another in mutual vulnerability. Members of a theatre group who had participated in the retreat summarized the whole affair by dramatizing the movements of prayer, community, and care.

Then everyone received a little colored paper heart. Nathan asked everyone to give their heart to someone else, lay hands on each other, and pray for one another. He said, "Just choose two or three people," but within a minute everyone was exchanging their little hearts with everyone else and blessing each other. It was beautiful to see the whole gymnasium filled with people giving their hearts to each other and praying for each other.

Then there were many thank-yous and many songs. Finally we held hands and danced in a long line from the gymnasium to the little parking lot outside, where we formed a large circle and kept singing "Alleluias" for another fifteen minutes.

Retreat in Rovesnyk camp. Fr Henri dressed in a heavy cassock.

Fr. Henri preaching, Borys translating.

After the retreat (August 1994).

Meanwhile, the buses were waiting to take people home. Vladzio was also there with the van to transport the people in wheelchairs and their mothers to Lviv. There was a lot of picture-taking, kissing, embracing, and waving goodbye. Then one by one the old and overloaded buses moved away, followed by Vladzio's van.

Zenia, Sue, Siobhan, Cheryl, Nathan, and I stayed behind, together with Theodore and about thirty of the retreatants, to spend the next two days on a workshop on servant leadership.

Monday, August 15, 1994

Last night all of us who stayed in Rovesnyk for the two-day workshop on servant leadership came together to pray, to introduce ourselves to each other in a more personal way than was possible during the large retreat, and to say what we wanted to learn. Most people were young women and men who belonged to Youth for Christ or Faith and Light. Their ages were between sixteen and twenty-five, with the exception of a few older people. Their lives were full of struggles in their families, their schools, and their work. All of them were hungry for an experience of safety, intimacy, and community, and a deep relationship with God. But all of them suffered from feelings of sinfulness, guilt, shame, low self-esteem, and distrust in others.

They wanted to learn how to pray, how to help others to pray, how to plan youth retreats, and how to create community for and with others. The retreat had been an incredible experience for them. Some said, "This was the most important spiritual experience of my life," or "This was the first time I felt loved and trusted," or "This was the first time that I realized that the spiritual life is basically a very simple thing." What they would have liked the most was that the retreat could have lasted much longer. They were happy to be in the workshop but they would have preferred to continue the experience of just being together praying, singing, listening to talks, and celebrating. They so seldom had a chance to be together that way, and they couldn't get enough of it.

We realized that these young people had more need for spiritual support, personal attention, and individual care than they had for leadership formation. They had many personal questions that we had not even touched on in the retreat: questions about their sexuality, about intimacy, about friendship, about their relationship with their parents, about finding some inner and outer space in their crowded lives, about their studies, their work, their vocation, their future. Endless questions. How could these people be asked to help others with such questions when they themselves never really had a chance to deal with them?

So the "workshop" needed to be something other than job training. It needed to be about ongoing spiritual formation with a few very elementary guidelines in offering leadership to others. When our team met last night after the evening session, we decided to spend the morning around the theme of "listening": listening to each other, listening to God.

Looking at leadership in church and society in Ukraine, it becomes obvious that leadership is seen as telling other people what to do. Political speeches and sermons are long and moralistic, and listening is certainly not on the agenda of many leaders. People are always talked at, warned, admonished, threatened, and even put down. Listening, as a way to receive another person and allow them to discover their own unique gifts, is unheard of in a world that has been subject to one dictatorship after another. To say that listening is a central quality of leadership is a very radical statement and nearly the opposite of what future leaders may expect to learn. Moreover, to think and speak about prayer as listening to God is no less radical. For so many people, God is not a safe God, but a controlling, manipulative, punishing, and vengeful God. Who wants to listen to such a God? For most Ukrainians the most important prayer is, "God have mercy on me, a sinner." It is a beautiful and very rich prayer, but it can also prevent people from wanting to be very close to God and to rest in God's embrace. If all I ask of God is mercy and forgiveness, how can I truly listen without fear and with a childlike trust?

This morning Father Myroslav Medvid celebrated the Eucharist in the little chapel at eight o'clock. I had seen Myroslav for a moment two nights ago and wondered who he was. He looked different from other priests: he was a strong, muscular man, without a beard and with short hair. He didn't wear a cassock or a collar, but sweatpants and a sport shirt. Two young men who behaved like bodyguards were with him. One of them held onto a racing bike. I asked Borys, "Who is this guy?" Borys told me the story. Now I know not only that he is the pastor of the Greek Catholic parish of the neighboring town of Chervonohrad, but also that in 1985 he created an uproar in the United States when he jumped from a Russian grain ship anchored in the Port of New Orleans trying to escape to the West. I vaguely remembered the incident that was in the newspapers at that time.

After the Eucharist, I asked if we could spend a little time together. He said, "I would love to. It would be an honor."

The workshop went very well. We talked about listening and did a series of exercises, we discussed the different elements that make up a retreat, we spent time in prayer, and we ended the day with a celebration carefully prepared by the five small teams: a welcoming team, a music team, a drama team, a homily team, and a celebration team. Two of the workshop members coordinated the different teams. It was a very beautiful evening: intimate, prayerful, gentle, and joyful. But when at the very end a song and a poem were presented in gratitude for us, the words reminded us of the very melancholy soul of Ukraine. There is a deep sadness in the heart of Ukrainian people, and even the prayers, hymns, and homilies that speak about hope and joy don't take that away easily—a thousand years of long-suffering, oppression, poverty, and the violent death of millions of people have engulfed this country in darkness—and words for darkness are easier to find than words for light.

Tuesday, August 16, 1994

After the Eucharist with Father Myroslav, Sue, Borys, and I had breakfast with him and were able to hear more about his journey. After having jumped from the ship and escaping to the "free world," the New Orleans police contacted the State Department. Orders soon came from them to send him back to his ship. Since it was only two weeks before President Reagan was going to meet Gorbachev for a summit, they didn't want any trouble with the Soviet Union at that time. But when Myroslav escaped for a second time by freeing himself from the guards who tried to bring him back to the ship, he became national news, and thousands of people, especially Ukrainians, protested against the State Department's decision. Senator Jesse Helms asked that Myroslav would at least be interviewed before the ship was allowed to leave the port. When this finally happened, Myroslav told the authorities that he had accidently fallen off the ship's deck and that he wanted to go back home. In fact, during the previous night he had had a profound religious experience and had decided not to ask for asylum but to return to his country.

When the ship came to Havana, the Soviet authorities took Myroslav off the ship, flew him to Ukraine, and put him in a psychiatric hospital. There, in the subsequent months, the KGB subjected him to more than seventy long, grueling interrogations. Since the political climate had changed under Gorbachev's perestroika, he was finally released. After that, he married and tried to be accepted into the Orthodox seminary, but the KGB kept harassing him and went so far as to try to make him an informer for them. During a stay in Moscow, he was even approached by some CIA agents who promised to get him into the seminary. But by that time Myroslav had become so disgusted with the political powers, whether from the East or West, that he withdrew from all government manipulation and went his own way until the end of the Soviet system gave him a chance to follow his vocation. A few years ago, he went to the seminary, became a Greek Catholic priest, and was appointed as pastor of Chervonohrad.

During our conversation, Myroslav showed me his left hand. "I gradually lost control over my left hand," he said. "The middle part is becoming numb and sometimes I have no sensation of touch there." He showed me his wrist, and I could see that it had been operated on. He said, "The operation was not quite successful. Here they do not have the microsurgical equipment needed to restore the circulation in my hand. I hope that someday, some surgeon in the West is able to help me. I feel it is quite urgent. I am afraid to lose the use of my hand. Sometimes during Mass I can't even feel the chalice I am holding."

"What happened?" I asked. He said, "I prefer not to talk about it." Borys said to me on the side, "The injury occurred during his ordeal with KGB authorities following the incident in New Orleans."

Speaking about his forced stay in the psychiatric institution, Myroslav said, "Happily there were a few good friends who helped me not to take the drugs they kept giving me. In that way I was able to keep my sanity." Myroslav still had fears of that terrible time. When we were standing outside, an older-looking man moved closer to us and appeared to be trying to overhear our conversation. Myroslav stopped talking and said, "Let's move away from him. That's one of the old KGB types."

Meeting Myroslav made me aware how much had happened within the last few years between New Orleans 1985 and Chervonohrad 1994. The world had become a very different place, and the enormous changes were summarized in the pain and joy of this merchant-marine-become-priest.

Myroslav joined us for the rest of the day. During the morning session we reflected on last evening's celebration and discussed again the three aspects of good planning: vision, tasks, and process. The emphasis this time was on process: how to move from here to there in the fulfillment of different tasks. The different work teams that had planned last night's evening reflected on the positive and negative experiences, and both Sue and Borys spoke about "processing" as an essential part of good planning.

During the second part of the morning I spoke about the prayer of Jesus in the midst of a very busy life of healing and proclamation, and tried to show how deep contemplative prayer that includes praise, thanksgiving, and intercession can help us to let go of our compulsiveness and to serve people in inner freedom. Cheryl and Siobhan helped members of the workshop to act out the Gospel stories in which it is told how Jesus was constantly bombarded by needy people but always found a quiet place to be alone with his heavenly father. During part of the event they sat in the center of the room like statues, signifying healing, proclamation, and prayer. I could just walk from one set of statues to the other to illustrate my thoughts. After this time, everyone went off by him- or herself for forty-five minutes of prayer, and shortly before lunch we gathered again for a period to share our experiences with God. It was very moving to listen to these young Ukrainians speaking with great love and conviction about the ways God had touched their hearts.

After lunch at 2:30, we met again for our closing service. Myroslav had invited the director of the camp to join us. It was the "dull, gray" man we had met on our arrival on Friday night! He was quite eager to come and expressed his desire to be better prepared for us when we came again. There were beautiful songs and prayer, and together we lifted up a large plate decorated with flowers on which each participant had placed a card telling how he or she planned to be servant leaders when they returned home. After many more songs, blessings, and thank-yous, we cleaned our rooms, packed our things, and waited for the buses to bring us home. Vladzio was already there with the van. At 4:30 we were on our way to Lviv.

We interrupted our trip with a short visit to the miraculous icon of Our Lady in the Basilian church in Chervonohrad. A beautiful old priest told us about the icon that had been taken to Poland during the Soviet period, but was recently returned. As he was telling the story he mentioned his ten years in the labor camps, his work in the underground Church, and the immense suffering of his people during this century. His simple but very penetrating words touched all of us and made us look at the icon with different eyes.

☩

Wednesday, August 17, 1994

After our four days at the camp, the Dnister Hotel felt like a great luxury. Everyone craved a quiet day with the freedom to do a few simple things. Later, during lunch, Zenia, Borys, Cheryl, Nathan, Sue, and I had a conversation about our experience at the retreat and workshop, and about ways to continue our involvement in Ukraine. It was clear to all of us that we had met many very talented young people with obvious leadership gifts, but it was also clear that without a lot of encouragement and guidance it would be hard for them to claim these gifts. We were all somewhat overwhelmed by the low self-esteem not only of individuals but also of the group as a whole. Some of the things we did, Ukrainians could do better, but still they didn't have the self-confidence needed to act on this truth.

At 5 p.m. we had a gentle Eucharistic celebration in Sue's room. Afterward, Vladzio drove all of us to the house of Theodore, his wife, Oksana, and their thirteen-year-old daughter, Orysia. It is also Borys's home. A beautiful dinner was prepared for us: soup, cheese and mushroom dumplings, cake, Jell-O, and ice cream, soft drinks, wine, brandy, and even champagne. It was a very festive and rich meal. Eight guests in a very small apartment. We hardly fit around the small table, and there was a lot of stepping over each other to move in and out, but what might be perceived as a problem in the West was a cause for joy in Lviv. We were close and happily together.

There were many words of gratitude. Theodore told us how depressed he was before we came and how our visit had started a new "epoch" for him. Borys explained how at very crucial moments of his life, friendship with me and other people had helped him through a critical time of decision and given him the support to move on in often uncertain directions. For him, our visit had been a real experience of love, support, encouragement, and healing. Nathan expressed our gratitude for the warm welcome to Theodore and Oksana's home and said that this intimate, festive evening would stay long in our memories as we returned to our lives in Canada.

For me personally, it was good to see Borys's little room in Theodore and Oksana's home. It was a scholar's room, with walls covered with bookshelves—all with double rows of books—with a bed, a desk, and a telephone. Now I know where Borys is when he calls me from Lviv early in the morning, which is late at night in Toronto.

Tomorrow will be our last day in Ukraine. I feel a little nervous about the large public lecture at the Polytechnical Institute in the evening—it will be the final event of our trip—I pray that all will go well.

Thursday, August 18, 1994

Last night Zenia received a phone call from her sister, who told her that her father's cancer could no longer be treated and that he might have only a short time left to live. Zenia realized that she had to go home as soon as possible to be with her father. Nathan, Sue, and I discussed with Zenia how we could best support her during her time back in Canada. At 4:30 we celebrated the Eucharist together. Zenia told us about the tears she had shed for her father and her desire to be with him in the weeks to come. We asked her to tell her father, when she called him tonight, that we all had celebrated the Eucharist together with many prayers for him and his family.

During the same celebration we all spoke about our experience during the last two weeks. Everyone expressed deep gratitude for the way we had lived this time together. On the way to the auditorium of the Polytechnical Institute, Borys and I went to the chancery office for a word of thanks to Father Ken Nowakowski, whose office had financially supported our stay. Father Ken is a Canadian from Saskatchewan who had worked for many years in Rome for Cardinal Lubachivsky and had come to Lviv with him as his head of staff and fundraiser. We had a good chat about fundraising, and the enormous challenges he faces.

"What about all the Ukrainians living in the West?" I asked. Father Ken smiled and said, they are quite generous, but bombarded with so many requests for money that they easily reach the limit of their ability to give. Moreover, many Ukrainians have hardly any close ties today with their home country and often feel more inclined to support more urgent needs in the world, such as the Rwanda refugees. It was interesting to have such a nuts-and-bolts discussion in a context where so few nuts and bolts can be seen.

At 6:30 we all gathered at the auditorium of the Polytechnical Institute. It was immediately clear that Youth for Christ had greatly overestimated our popularity. The auditorium could hold eleven hundred people. Not more than three hundred showed up. The main excuse for the low attendance was that the organizers had failed to take into consideration that tomorrow is the Feast of the Transfiguration, one of the main feast days in the Greek Catholic Church. The evening before, in all churches, the Vespers of the feast were celebrated. What priest would announce an event in the Polytechnical Institute that would conflict with the Vespers in his own church?

But, small as the audience was, it was a joyful evening. There was good singing, and both Sue and I spoke with as much enthusiasm as we could muster up. People listened with great attention. When I spoke about mourning our losses and enumerated the many losses the Ukrainian people had suffered, I saw tears in the listeners' eyes, especially among the older people. As I walked up and down the aisles in the auditorium I could see the immense pain and suffering on people's faces. I realize how important it is to name the pain and to speak about healing without in any way denying the context of despair.

During the mime the actors moved from the stage into the auditorium, laying hands on each individual person in the audience. People were deeply touched. After the mime, a man in the audience came to the microphone and spoke about the need for healing and forgiveness.

"Fellow countrymen," he said, "after years in a labor camp, I came home to my village. Everything was destroyed, many friends and family members had been killed. I cannot forgive the system that caused all the destruction, but God asked me to forgive those who did the destroying and the killing. It is hard, but I must forgive and thus maintain my human dignity." As he spoke, tears came to his eyes, and twice he choked on his emotions and was unable to speak.

There were also many written questions: "Why didn't you start this meeting with prayer?" "How can I live in peace with people who constantly harass me?" "What is the worst sin, and does God forgive all sins?" "What is your impression of Ukraine after your two weeks here?" I tried to respond as well as possible. Then we concluded with prayer, and for half an hour after that, many stayed around singing, clapping, and finally dancing through the aisles.

Friday, August 19, 1994

This morning we all met to celebrate the Feast of the Transfiguration and to pray for each other, our communities, Ukraine, and the world. It was a very simple and very prayerful Eucharist.

At 10 a.m. Lubomyr and Hryhoriy, the two drivers who had taken us from Warsaw to Lviv, were waiting for us in their Volkswagen bus. We all said goodbye to Borys, who had to give a television interview about the Union of Brest. It was very hard for me to depart from Borys. I love him deeply, and our friendship had grown much deeper and stronger during the last fourteen days. I realized that Borys was going to have a very busy time in the next month. I wished I could offer him more support in the days ahead, but I trust that he will continue to draw strength from our time together. In October, he will be going to Rome for a year, to get a licentiate in theology to finish his book on the Union of Brest, and to explore in more depth an ecclesiology that could help him to live well in the Greek Catholic Church. I am thinking of ways to support him in the coming year. Should I go to Rome? Should he come to Toronto? We will see. As I embraced him I realized how deeply grateful I am to have him as a lifelong friend.

A little group of Faith and Light friends was waiting for us in the reception area of the hotel to say their goodbyes. Outside as we got ready to enter the bus, Vasyl sang the Ave Maria in his beautiful counter-tenor voice. He made his sung prayer heard all through the square in front of the hotel. We said goodbye to Siobhan, Marguerite, Zenia, and all our other friends. Theodore decided to come with us to help us with the border crossing. "How is he going to get back?" I asked. "Oh, don't worry, he will take a bus," they said. I realized how caring and generous Theodore was.

We stopped at the marketplace to buy some food, and at 11 a.m. we were on our way to Warsaw. At the border we had the usual "ceremonies." This time no cassock and rosary, but only the letter of the cardinal and Theodore showing the newspaper with my photograph. One of the Ukrainian border police immediately came up to me for an autograph!

The Polish border police were a little less cooperative, but with the help of the two drivers and Theodore, we got through within forty-five minutes—a lot faster than many of the other cars.

At the first little town beyond the border, Theodore said goodbye to us and left us to return to Lviv. It would be a long, busy trip for him with a long wait at the border!

We arrived at 7 p.m. at the Gromada Hotel in Warsaw. Compared with the Dnister Hotel in Lviv, the Gromada Hotel was pure luxury. Nice soap, large towels, warm water, and all the other little luxuries of the West. We offered our drivers a room. "No, no," they said. "We will sleep in the bus." But it had become very cold and we insisted. After one more refusal, they finally accepted. "We have never stayed in a hotel," they said. We invited them for dinner, but they preferred their own way of eating.

Being back in Poland was like being back in the West. As we drove into Warsaw and saw the well-stocked stores, the well-dressed people, and the well-run transportation system, we became aware of Ukraine's poverty. Not only were there many poor people in Ukraine, but Ukraine as a nation was poor, poorly situated in Europe, poorly treated by East and West, poorly held together by conflicting political interests. Being in Poland made me aware that Ukraine is like the foster child of Europe, not highly respected, not well supported, not given the attention it needs.

I suddenly remembered that in the story of the Last Judgment, God judges not individuals, but nations. The question "What have you done to the least of mine?" does not simply refer to individual poor people but also, and maybe first of all, to poor nations. God loves the poor; God even has a preferential love for the poor. Ukraine is poor, very poor, not just materially, but also emotionally and spiritually. To care for the poor means much more than to reach out to people who need food, jobs, clothes, and a safe place to stay. It means also to care for nations that are crushed by the forces of history and live under the burden of being ignored and rejected by the international community.

As we were eating our quite copious dinner at the restaurant of the Gromada Hotel, we reflected on our experience in Ukraine. Personally I felt a deep desire to stay faithful to the Ukrainian people and to keep choosing not just for the individual poor, who need support, but also for the country that is so clearly marginalized in the family of nations.

Saturday, August 20, 1994

At 5:50 a.m. the hotel taxi took us to the Warsaw Airport. At 7:10 a.m. we left on a Delta flight to Prague and flew from there to Frankfurt. At 11 a.m., after a change of planes in Frankfurt, we were on our way to New York's John F. Kennedy Airport.

One thing that struck us all as we traveled west was that the people seemed less and less somber. The people who came on board in Prague seemed a little more playful than the people who had boarded the plane with us in Warsaw, and the people at the Frankfurt Airport, passengers as well as gate personnel, were more talkative and easygoing than the people from Prague. Some of this may be just projection, an expression of our desire to go home and see in people some of what we hope to find when we are finally back in Toronto. Still, the journey from Ukraine to Poland, to Germany, and then to the United States made us aware that our own emotions and feelings about who we are and what we are able to do are very much connected to the social, economic, political, and religious structures that have molded our hearts and our minds.

Within an hour, we will be back in Toronto. It has been a very long day, but a good day, full of gratitude and full of hope.

ॐ

Sunday, August 21, 1994

Yesterday certainly was the longest day of my life. We got up at 5 a.m. in Warsaw and went to bed at 2 a.m. in Toronto (8 a.m. in Warsaw). It is good to be back; we are tired but very satisfied.

Nathan and I decided to spend Sunday together in the apartment of a friend who was spending the month of August in Japan. Thus we could sleep a lot, pray, and write a little before reentering the busy life of the Daybreak community.

The apartment we are staying at has all the luxuries of our Western technological society: air conditioning, microwave, stereo set, washer and dryer, and well-equipped kitchen and bathrooms. After our time in Ukraine all of these facilities were no longer as typical as they had seemed. When we walked in the supermarket the enormous choice of food offered was in stark contrast to the empty shelves in Lviv. Even though planes make the physical distances between Ukraine and Canada seem small, the socioeconomic, spiritual, and emotional distance is still enormous. I am committed to keep working to bridge this gap.

When Nathan and I were telling our stories last night to Kathy Bruner, a longtime member of our community, we became aware that telling our story to our friends was one important way of bridge-building. We so quickly forget how spoiled we are and how much we take for granted. Although we live and work with people with mental handicaps, we certainly do not live a poor life. Our trips to Ukraine show us another type of handicap. It is the handicap that comes from a broken history, from centuries of oppression and exploitation, from neglect and indifference of the wealthy nations, from the social sins of injustice and greed. Not only people with mental handicaps are marginalized in our world, but countries as well. Ukraine is one of the marginalized countries among the international community of nations. Men and women with mental handicaps in Ukraine are the marginalized people in a marginalized country. I trust that the connection between the Daybreak community in Toronto and the Faith and Light communities in Lviv is a blessed connection: blessed not just for the parents and their children with handicaps in Ukraine, but blessed, too, for us in the West who have as much to receive as to give.

"Blessed are the poor," Jesus says. He does not say, "Blessed are those who give to the poor." The true blessing comes from the poor. After this trip to Ukraine I know in a new way that the people we have met there challenge us to be faithful to our commitment to the poor and to trust that through that faithfulness we will find true joy and peace.

Afterword

Twenty-Nine Years Later

Dear Henri,

I must write to you.

In the early morning of February 24, 2022, all hell broke loose in Ukraine. The invaders came from the north, the east, and from the south. Ukraine burned like the edges of a book thrown into the fire. Armored iron rolled in a thousand-fold. Rockets sliced through the blue sky and slammed into apartment buildings, hospitals, and anywhere else. Heavy artillery bombed randomly day and night. Ukraine was fully hit in its face.

Now, six months later, the battle rages on relentlessly. Cities are ruined. Thousands of people, young and old, have been killed, tens of thousands maimed for life, millions left in despair, homeless, or on the run. How much destruction, how many deaths and injuries, how much inhumanity still awaits the people of Ukraine?

Henri, so often you sang the Taizé song: "Ubi Caritas et Amor deus ibi est" (Where there is care and love for one another, there is God). It made me believe that the divine could exist. Now, in Mariupol, Bucha, and all those raped villages, I hear and see nothing but the opposite.

Why must I write this to you, dear brother? What is the point of writing to a brother who died years ago, in 1996? I do not know. Nor do I know why I am still in silent conversation with our father and mother, often in my dreams, often when I sit still and look out over the river that flows slowly westward. How long has it been since they died? I am now old, struggling with cancer, with my life's horizon within sight. During your life you were older brother by twelve years; now I find myself fourteen years older than the age you were granted in life. But what does that matter? The bond with our parents, with our siblings, family members, and friends remains. I am with them beyond the limits of the temporal. Does the boundary between those on this side and those on the other blur as we age? So now I must share with you my sorrow over the disaster that has befallen our friends in Ukraine. It was you, after all, who sent me there.

It was twenty-nine years ago in 1993 that you first visited Lviv, Ukraine, followed by a second trip the following year. You wrote two diaries about your visits. You were deeply moved by the hardship of poverty, the low self-esteem, the suffering of the Ukrainians. The message you delivered to your traumatized and victimized audience was hard for them to believe: "Above all: You are the beloved sons and daughters of God. The same is said to you and each of you as was said to Jesus by the Spirit when baptized in the Jordan River." How, after centuries of war, slavery, and persecution, could they accept this message of being beloved? "Lord have mercy" was their centuries-old chorus in response to all the deep history of pain and tears. Nevertheless, they came to listen to you, desperately wanting to believe your message.

The invitation to Ukraine came from Borys Gudziak and Zenia Kushpeta. Borys was your friend and student from your time as a professor at Harvard Divinity School. Zenia was your colleague in the L'Arche Daybreak community where you had gone to live and work. Both Borys and Zenia were children born in the diaspora. Their parents had fled Soviet Ukraine following the Second World War. Both Borys and Zenia returned to Ukraine shortly after its independence in 1991. Borys went in response to a call to support the recovery of the Ukrainian Greek Catholic Church, which had been severely persecuted and almost destroyed by the Communist regime. Zenia went to carry the message of Daybreak and to establish homes and safe places for the very many disabled people who had been totally neglected and deprived of any human dignity during the long Soviet era.

Henri, you did not go to Ukraine as a tourist or just to meet some friends. You went with a new vision that started when you gave up your prestigious status as a professor at Harvard, a vision that deepened in the humble community of Daybreak. It was there that you met your "teacher," the severely handicapped man Adam. And it was through him that you were able to meet the Ukrainians, so wounded by their dramatic history, and so much the "orphans" in the family of nations.

At the age of fifty-four, when you left Harvard and gave up being professor, you told me, "I realized in my heart that the way of the gospel is actually the other way round, a downward-going way, a more downward walking way, to the places of weakness, to the places of poverty, to the places of brokenness, while I was actually climbing up to the places of power, strength, and influence. I began to experience the tension between that upward and downward movement very strongly inwardly. Then I thought, *I have to do something else. I have to choose for my vocation that way that always invites me to go down, down in the sense of going to places where people are poor, where people are weak and often sad.*" That was the beginning of your downward path to Daybreak. And further down the path you would eventually reach Ukraine.

All your life you had struggled with the question of how to follow Christ and how to live as a beloved child of God. While you were still a professor at Yale Divinity School, you took a break and ventured to live as a contemplative monk. But after six months living a strict monastic life you realized you were not contemplative enough for such a life. Some years later you tried again "to follow Christ" by going to Bolivia and Peru to live with the poor in the slums of Lima. But you were not practically skilled to be of any use for these needy poor, and after six months you returned to be a bridge between the poor of Latin America and the rich of North America. But despite these frustrating experiences, you were not discouraged from continuing your search for a way to follow Christ and to keep alive your vocation to live as God's beloved.

The decision to give up "all and everything" to move to Daybreak was not easy. Your family and friends had advised you not to abandon a position at Harvard, where you could do so much more than at this unknown place with handicapped people in Canada. But the invitation from Sue Mosteller of L'Arche Daybreak was stronger and ultimately irresistible. She said, "We cannot offer you a salary, but only a home." And so you went.

You must have been nervous and insecure taking this step on the way down. Would this new venture last longer than six months? Not suitable as a monk, not suitable in the slums, would you find yourself suited to a community with handicapped people?

Immediately after your arrival in the community, you were assigned to take care of Adam, a severely handicapped young man. Adam was deaf, he could not speak, he was wheelchair-bound and constantly plagued by epileptic seizures. You had to wake him up in the morning, dress him, brush his teeth, feed him, and be with him all day. There is no greater contrast imaginable between your audience in the packed lecture halls of Harvard and this severely disabled and speechless man.

You were afraid of Adam, his spastic movements and deep growls. You felt completely incapable of taking care of him. But the community asked you to be patient, and Adam was also patient with you. It did not matter to Adam that you had been a professor, that you were a celebrated writer and much sought-after speaker. He just needed your full attention and care.

Family, friends, and L'Arche Daybreak community members
after Fr. Henri Nouwen's funeral (September 28, 1996).

I'm sure you wouldn't have lasted long at Daybreak if it had not been for Adam and all that he taught you. As you later wrote, "Adam's gift is that he has a heart that loves and is loved. And what makes him human is not so much whether he can talk or not talk, but that he has a heart with which he can give love and receive love. Adam is the one who also taught me to know God in a very, very intimate way. Adam doesn't argue, Adam doesn't have opinions, but Adam is someone who in his weakness reveals God to us in a very gentle way." You came to understand that Adam had a mission for all of us. Adam was truly a peacemaker: "Adam, in his weakness and in his search for help, asks all people around him to be good to each other. He is saying to you: I can live if you love each other. Your love is necessary for me to live well. If we do not get along well, he will not make it well. And actually that is the deepest bond of our being together."

I realize now that it was your experience at Daybreak and your encounter with Adam that prepared you for the invitation from Ukraine. That experience totally restructured your vision of Christ and the presence of the divine. It was a true experience of conversion. Now, so many decades later, I realize that Daybreak is not an isolated place for handicapped people, but that Daybreak is as large as our whole world, a community of handicapped humanity. And I now realize that Adam, the man you had to care for, was not a marginalized person, but a missionary. Now I understand that Daybreak includes Ukraine and that Ukrainians are very much the Adams in our present violent world. Now I understand how the severely handicapped and wounded people of Ukraine reveal, in their weakness and vulnerability, the suffering of God's beloved yet crucified children. Now I understand how Ukraine today is another Adam, telling the world it can only survive if all powerful nations love each other and live in peace.

It was shortly after your totally unexpected death in 1996 that I found your Ukrainian diaries. There was one short sentence in them that changed my comfortable life: "There is the desire to get a typewriter and electric wheelchair for Andriy. All this will certainly happen." You wrote these words on August 14, 1993. That day you had met Andriy, a very talented poet, suffering from cerebral palsy and not able to write by hand. How did you know that all this would certainly happen? Let me tell you what did happen. Maybe you know, maybe not. God only knows what the dead know.

*For twenty 20 years the Henri Nouwen Foundation regularly
brought humanitarian aid to Ukraine. His brother Laurent
passed an exam to be able to drive a track. (2011).*

You visited Ukraine a second time in 1994 and again
you wrote daily in your second diary. Yes, you visited Andriy
and his friends from Faith and Light again, but you had not
brought him his typewriter. You never were very practical, and
probably you had no clue how to get a typewriter from Canada
through customs into Ukraine.

But in reading that one sentence I realized that you were
telling me to make it happen. In 1997 I brought Andriy his
typewriter, and in doing so I saw how many young men and
women there were like Andriy and how great their needs
were. We established the Henri Nouwen Foundation, through
which, over more than twenty-five years, we were able to

support Ukrainians in desperate orphanages for abandoned children and in psychiatric hospitals, which were no more than filthy dumping sites for marginalized people. We could support educational reforms, family care, and shelters for the homeless. Over those years, with a group of volunteers and loyal donors, we could deliver over 120 truckloads of goods, and over twenty minibuses for the transport of isolated handicapped people. And we were able to provide financial funding for initiatives by young and caring Ukrainians—many of whom had been in your audiences—for social justice, solidarity, and human dignity. Your words—"You are invited to live the life of the beloved"—became the inspiration for many Ukrainians to rise up from passive depression to positive action.

All our help would have been in vain if we had not had the opportunity to work with young Ukrainians who, with enormous dedication, would transfer the persistent narrative of being victim at all times into a narrative of "Yes we can" and "Yes we will." It was Vitaliy Kokor who tirelessly managed to implement our efforts to improve the lives of the marginalized. It was Vitaliy who then managed to build the nongovernmental organization Ukrainian Education Platform into a great voluntary organization with hundreds of social projects all over Ukraine. Later, it was Roksolana and Natalya who meticulously and energetically made our projects possible by serving as our representatives on the ground.

Following in your footsteps, I have visited the beautiful city of Lviv in western Ukraine, perhaps a hundred times or more. In September 2021, the twenty-fifth anniversary of your death, I visited for what was probably the last time in my life. Once again, I went into the lobby of the hotel where you stayed during your visits in 1993 and 1994 and where Borys told you and your companions so much about the history of Ukraine and where you and Zenia and her friends prayed and celebrated the Eucharist.

So much has changed since then. With tremendous and everlasting energy, Borys Gudziak and his friends were able not only to restore the Lviv Theological Academy but to develop the institute into the vibrant, internationally renowned, state-of-the-art, Ukrainian Catholic University. Zenia and her friends were able not only to establish L'Arche Ukraine with various daycare centers for the handicapped but also to create the Dzherelo Center, a highly sophisticated rehabilitation and educational center, unique for Ukraine and a nationwide example for care of the handicapped.

Henri, thank you for visiting Ukraine twenty-nine years ago, thank you for giving me Andriy and many other good friends, thanks for your diaries, thanks for making my life worthwhile, thank you for your never-forsaken belief that we all are free as beloved sons and daughters of God.

As evil once again seeks to destroy Ukraine and reduce it to smoldering ashes, I know that your encouragement that we all are free as beloved sons and daughters of God still lives on in the courage of men and women in Ukraine, standing up in defense of their poor, wounded country.

On Friday, August 19, 1994, at the very end of your second visit to Ukraine, you reflected, "Not only were there many poor people in Ukraine, but Ukraine as a nation was poor, poorly situated in Europe, poorly treated by East and West, poorly held together by conflicting political interests. Being in Poland made me aware that Ukraine is like the foster child of Europe, not highly respected, not well supported, not given the attention it needs. I suddenly remembered that in the story of the Last Judgment, God judges not individuals, but nations. The question 'What have you done to the least of mine?' does not simply refer to individual poor people but also, and maybe first of all, to poor nations. God loves the poor, God even has a preferential love for the poor. Ukraine is poor, very poor, not just materially, but also emotionally and spiritually. To care for the poor means much more than to reach out to people who need food, jobs, clothes, and a safe place to stay. It means also to care for nations that are crushed by the forces of history and live under the burden of being ignored and rejected by the international community.... Personally I felt a deep desire to stay faithful to the Ukrainian people and to keep choosing not just for the individual poor, who need support, but also for the country that is so clearly marginalized in the family of nations."

Henri, twenty-nine years later, your words are as true and as relevant as ever.

Laurent Nouwen
August 2022